THE
COUNTESS

BY
GREGORY MURPHY

★

★

DRAMATISTS
PLAY SERVICE
INC.

THE COUNTESS
Copyright © 2000, Gregory Murphy

All Rights Reserved

2

for my parents
Helen Glasco Murphy and James M. Murphy

ACKNOWLEDGMENT

Gregory Murphy would like to thank Mr. Robert Parks and the Pierpont Morgan Library in New York for having made The Bowerswell Papers available to him in his research on *The Countess*.

HISTORICAL BACKGROUND OF *THE COUNTESS*

In London in 1848, three very idealistic, young artists, John Everett Millais, Dante Gabriel Rossetti, and William Holman Hunt banded together to form the Pre-Raphaelite Brotherhood. The goal of the Pre-Raphaelites, or the PRB as they called themselves, was to emulate the simple feeling and naive, unadorned directness of painting as it existed prior to the Renaissance. The three wanted to throw off the stifling influence of the Renaissance, and at the same time challenge the power of the Royal Academy. The Academy, under Sir Joshua Reynolds, had established a series of guidelines which all English artists were effectively compelled to follow. This code called for the emphasis of shadow over light, muted tones over vivid coloring, and the idealization of landscapes and people (as well as their clothing and very attitudes) in all painting.

For the Pre-Raphaelites truth to nature was to be art's only guideline. They scorned the artificiality of Academy art, and when their brilliantly colored, naturalistic paintings with the cryptic PRB monogram began to appear in London in 1850, they shocked and perplexed the art establishment. Further, when the identity and extreme youth (all were in their early twenties) of the artists was discovered, there was a firestorm of outrage. They were wrongly accused of mocking Raphael's genius, excoriated for their disregard of academic ideals of beauty, and ridiculed for treating their subjects with uncompromising realism. Charles Dickens, offended that Millais would presume to portray the Virgin Mary as an ordinary middle-aged woman, wrote furiously that Millais had painted her so that "she would stand out as a monster among her sisters in the vilest cabaret in France or the lowest gin shop in England."

John Ruskin, the foremost art critic in Victorian England, stood virtually alone in his defense of the Pre-Raphaelites — championing them in letter after letter to the *Times*. Ruskin admired the youthful energy and enthusiasm of the Pre-Raphaelites. Besides, the Pre-Raphaelite philosophy of truth to nature closely conformed to his own, as is apparent from his famous dictum to "go to nature in all singleness of heart and walk with her laboriously and trustingly, adding nothing, rejecting nothing, scorning nothing." With Ruskin as their defender the Pre-Raphaelites were able to survive and eventually to flourish.

In 1853, Ruskin invited John Everett Millais to join him and his wife Effie on a four-month holiday in the Scottish Highlands. Millais readily agreed. In addition to being greatly indebted to Ruskin for his vigorous defense of the Pre-Raphaelites, Millais idolized the older (by ten years) man for his brilliance and learning. The trip to Scotland was intended to seal the growing friendship between the two men, and to afford Millais the opportunity to paint Ruskin's portrait. The Ruskins and Millais settled into a small cottage in the Highland town of Brig o'Turk in mid-July 1853, and Millais was soon writing happily to his friend Holman Hunt of his "kind, forbearing" host and his pretty young wife, "the most delightful companion one could wish."

As the months passed, however, Millais' letters took on a more critical tone. His mild, ethereal host confounded him completely. Ruskin's mind he wrote seemed "always in the clouds and out of the reach of ordinary mortals." Mrs. Ruskin was, however, still charming. Soon almost all mention of Mrs. Ruskin disappeared from his letters, and when Ruskin was spoken of at all, it was often in scorn. Eventually Millais would write of the man he had once so admired: "I can scarcely trust myself to speak of Ruskin, who certainly appears to me to be the most wicked man I have known in my life. This I say without hesitation and methodically." But by then Everett Millais was, as his brother later wrote, "hopelessly and senselessly in love" with John Ruskin's beautiful young wife.

The Ruskins and Millais returned to London in December of 1853. Millais, obsessed with Effie Ruskin, decided that he had to get away from London, and made plans to leave for Cairo to paint for several years in the Holy Lands. Before he was to leave, Millais wrote to Effie's parents that their daughter was being grossly mistreated by Ruskin and urged them to act on her behalf. Almost simultaneously, Effie Ruskin's very good friend Lady Elizabeth Eastlake (renowned writer and essayist of the period) began to observe the rapid deterioration of her friend's emotional state. Lady Eastlake pressed Effie until she learned the truth at the core of the Ruskin marriage — that it had never been consummated. Ruskin, unable to have relations with his bride on their wedding night, worked to convince his young wife (she was nineteen at the time of their marriage) that his failure was due to the fact that she was physically repugnant — that she had "an internal disease," and although possessed of a beautiful face, had a body which "was not formed to excite passion." He further tried to convince her, and seemed in fact convinced himself, that she was mentally ill — a belief in which his parents, who detested Effie for what they saw as her efforts to separate them from their son, supported him.

Lady Eastlake assisted Effie as she secretly prepared to leave Ruskin. The evening of her departure, Ruskin was served with papers to nullify their marriage. Ruskin's parents were appalled to learn their son's marriage had never been consummated, but rallied to his side against his former wife. His father sought to have Effie attacked in court as mentally unbalanced, until his own solicitor was forced to point out to him that the court might view the rather "unusual circumstances" of the marriage as having perhaps contributed to any mental disorder she might suffer. Effie's flight from Ruskin created a notorious scandal in London, which persisted through the lifetimes of all three participants.

Effie married Millais after her marriage to Ruskin was annulled, and had eight children with him. "Let me say at once," their son John wrote years later of their wedding day, "how much my father's future happiness was due to the chief event of this day." On his deathbed, Everett Millais (by then Lord Millais, aged sixty-seven, and the most popular artist in England) was asked by Queen Victoria if there was anything she might do for him. After Effie had left Ruskin, Queen Victoria had barred her from society. For years Millais had pressed the Queen to receive his wife back into society, something she adamantly refused to do. Millais' final request to the Queen was once again that she receive his wife. The Queen at last relented and received Effie Millais at court. Millais died shortly after and was honored by burial in St. Paul's Cathedral.

Ruskin never remarried after Effie left him, but went on to write some of his greatest work, including, in addition to his criticism on art and architecture, essays on religion, science, politics and philosophy. Several years after the dissolution of his marriage, Ruskin became wildly infatuated with nine-year-old Rose LaTouche (Effie's approximate age when Ruskin became enamored of her). Ruskin waited until Rose turned eighteen, then proposed to her, but her parents stepped in to prevent the marriage. Throughout his life, Ruskin (like Lewis Carroll) was almost exclusively attracted to young girls, leading many to theorize that his difficulties with his wife were due to his never having progressed beyond early adolescence emotionally. Ruskin suffered several severe nervous breakdowns before finally going completely mad the last ten years of his life. After he died, the love letters Effie had written to him before their marriage were found hidden beneath a floorboard in his house.

—Gregory Murphy

THE COUNTESS was originally produced by Ludovica Villar-Hauser in association with Paul Leyden and Marnee May as a sixteen-performance showcase at the Greenwich Street Theatre in New York in December 1995. Two staged readings of the play followed at the Pinter Theatre in London in September 1996 and March 1997. The play, produced by the Villar-Hauser Theatre Development Fund in association with Marnee May and Leatha Sturges, premiered at the Greenwich Street Theatre on March 14, 1999. After a successful two-month run there, THE COUNTESS transferred Off-Broadway to the Samuel Beckett Theatre where it celebrated its three-hundredth performance on February 9, 2000. It was directed by Ludovica Villar-Hauser; the set design was by Mark Symczak; the lighting design was by Stewart Wagner and Carrie Sophia Hash; the costume design was by Chris Lione and Elizabeth F.K. Muxi; the original music was by Dewey Dellay; and the production stage managers were Shan Bryant, Andrew John Tucker and Ci Herzog. The cast was as follows:

MARGARET RUSKIN .... Honora Fergusson
LADY ELIZABETH EASTLAKE .... Kristin Griffith
JOHN EVERETT MILLAIS .... Jy Murphy
JOHN RUSKIN, SR. .... Frederick Neumann
FREDERICK CRAWLEY .... John Quilty
JOHN RUSKIN .... James Riordan
EFFIE RUSKIN .... Jennifer Woodward

ALTERNATES FOR
MARGARET RUSKIN AND JOHN RUSKIN, SR.
Anita Keal, Richard Seff

OFFSTAGE VOICES
Angela Scowen
Victor Villar-Hauser

UNDERSTUDIES
Jennifer Donlin
Mike Finesilver

CAST OF CHARACTERS

EUPHEMIA CHALMERS GRAY RUSKIN
("EFFIE" or "COUNTESS")
Beautiful young wife of John Ruskin. Age 25.

JOHN RUSKIN
Preeminent nineteenth-century art critic. Age 35.

JOHN EVERETT MILLAIS
Painter and one of the founders of the Pre-Raphaelite
movement in England. Age 25.

JOHN JAMES RUSKIN
John Ruskin's father. A very successful
wine merchant. Age 68.

MARGARET RUSKIN
John Ruskin's mother. Age 72.

LADY ELIZABETH EASTLAKE
Writer and London friend of Euphemia Ruskin. Age 45.

FREDERICK CRAWLEY
John and Euphemia Ruskin's servant. Age 18.

Voices

SETTING

PROLOGUE

ACT ONE
Scene 1 — London. The Royal Academy.
Scene 2 — London. The drawing room at Denmark Hill,
the home of John James Ruskin. June 21, 1853.
Scene 3 — Brig o'Turk, Scotland. Schoolmaster
Alex Stewart's cottage. July 9, 1853.
Scene 4 — July 10, 1853.
Scene 5 — Mid-August 1853.
Scene 6 — Mid-September 1853.
Scene 7 — Afternoon. Late October 1853.
Scene 8 — Evening. Late October 1853.

ENTR'ACTE

ACT TWO
Scene 1 — Edinburgh. The Philosophical Institution.
November 1853.
Scene 2 — London. The drawing room at Denmark Hill.
Late December 1853.
Scene 3 — Early January 1854.
Scene 4 — April 13, 1854.
Scene 5 — Afternoon. April 14, 1854.
Scene 6 — Morning. April 25, 1854.
Scene 7 — Evening. April 25, 1854.

EPILOGUE

THE COUNTESS

PROLOGUE

1ST VOICE. The Queen — Victoria — wishes to know if there is anything she might now do for your father?

2ND VOICE. Yes. He wants that the Queen should receive his wife before he dies.

1ST VOICE. Impossible! The scandal.

2ND VOICE. Forty years ago!

1ST VOICE. It is notorious yet.

2ND VOICE. Is it possible the Queen cannot know how deeply Father has felt Her Majesty's having so barred his wife from society all these years?

1ST VOICE. If there is anything else which —

2ND VOICE. That is his request. His only request of Her Majesty.

ACT ONE

Scene 1

John Ruskin, the preeminent nineteenth-century art critic, age 35, is giving a farewell speech before The Royal Academy before departing on a four-month trip to Scotland with his wife, Effie, and his protégé and friend, the Pre-Raphaelite painter John Everett Millais.

RUSKIN. The especial condition of true ornament is that it be beautiful in its place, and nowhere else, that it not by its richness make other parts bland, or by its delicacy others coarse. So, members of the Academy, as I prepare to depart for the wilds of Scotland — with my perhaps even wilder young friend. *(Laughter.)* I advise each of you to go — for you have been too long from her, and all she might teach you — to Venice. That ghost upon the sands of the sea — so weak — so quiet — so bereft of all but her loveliness, that you might well doubt as you watch her faint reflection in the mirage of the lagoon, which is the city and which the shadow. *(Wild applause.)*

Scene 2

Lights up. A stage set with a few props to suggest the drawing room at Denmark Hill, the South London home of John James Ruskin, a wealthy wine merchant. It is June 21, 1853. Sitting in the room are Mr. Ruskin, age sixty-eight; his wife Margaret, age seventy-two; and their son John.

MR. RUSKIN. Has the world gone mad? Why must it be for so many months, John?
MRS. RUSKIN. Yes, John, why so long a time? And the Highlands. With your susceptibility to the damp.
RUSKIN. I will not listen to this. You knew from the first how long we would be gone. Besides, you see how much better Effie's been, planning and packing.
MR. RUSKIN. And when she returns?
MRS. RUSKIN. I will fret so for her, all the while you're gone.
MR. RUSKIN. In a month or two, John. Perhaps when she feels better.
RUSKIN. We leave for Scotland today. You must trust me. I know my wife.
MRS. RUSKIN. Where is she?
RUSKIN. Gone to bid farewell to Elizabeth Eastlake.
MRS. RUSKIN. But Lady Eastlake ... *(The Ruskin's servant*

Frederick Crawley, age eighteen, enters.)
CRAWLEY. Lady Eastlake, sir.
MRS. RUSKIN. John, I distinctly told you Lady Eastlake would be by this morning to say goodbye to Effie.
RUSKIN. Mother, I forgot. Please, would you deal with her? *(Lady Eastlake enters. She is a tall, aristocratic woman of forty-five. Crawley exits.)*
LADY EASTLAKE. Good morning.
MRS. RUSKIN. Lady Eastlake, I fear I've made a terrible mistake.
LADY EASTLAKE. Oh?
MRS. RUSKIN. I neglected to tell Effie of your plans, and I fear she's at your home in Fitzroy Square this very moment to bid you goodbye.
LADY EASTLAKE. How disappointing.
RUSKIN. Lady Eastlake, we're to leave momentarily for King's Cross Station. Effie's to meet us there. You will join us?
LADY EASTLAKE. Yes. Thank you, John.
MR. RUSKIN. Lady Eastlake, I just finished your essay in *The Quarterly*. Remarkable.
LADY EASTLAKE. Did you think so?
RUSKIN. Your tongue no doubt in your cheek.
LADY EASTLAKE. Actually, I had hoped to place it rather more prominently.
RUSKIN. The Photographic Society can not have been pleased.
LADY EASTLAKE. Only insofar as they fancy themselves artists.
MRS. RUSKIN. I begin to despair I should ever understand lady writers.
LADY EASTLAKE. I would not have you vex yourself, Madam. And so needlessly. *(Crawley enters.)*
CRAWLEY. Mr. Millais, sir. *(Everett Millais, a twenty-five-year-old artist of growing renown, flies into the room. Crawley exits.)*
MILLAIS. Good morning! Are we off then?
RUSKIN. Ready for the great Scottish adventure, Everett?
MILLAIS. I'm on fire for it!
LADY EASTLAKE. And this combustible young man is?
RUSKIN. Pardon me, Lady Eastlake. May I present Mr. Everett Millais.

MILLAIS. How do you do? Please to give Sir Charles my regards.

LADY EASTLAKE. So, I finally meet the prodigy. I suppose you know how fond Sir Charles is of you.

MILLAIS. And, I him. So. Where is the Countess?

LADY EASTLAKE. The Countess?

RUSKIN. My wife. *(Lady Eastlake looks surprised.)*

MILLAIS. In the Highlands, Lady Eastlake, we might call ourselves anything we like.

LADY EASTLAKE. And you, Mr. Millais, are to be a duke, perhaps.

MILLAIS. King.

LADY EASTLAKE. The Highlands indeed.

MILLAIS. So, is your wife intent on driving us all mad doing her last-minute woman things?

RUSKIN. She's somewhere now, I should think, between Fitzroy Square and King's Cross Station.

MILLAIS. What?

RUSKIN. I'll explain on the way. We'll miss our train, if we don't leave at once.

MRS. RUSKIN. John.

RUSKIN. Everything will be all right, Mother. Shall we go? *(The Ruskins depart. Lady Eastlake detains Millais.)*

LADY EASTLAKE. Mr. Millais, I — *(Lady Eastlake seems to want to say something to Millais, but decides against it.)* I hope you all have a wonderful time.

MILLAIS. Oh, I say! We're going to eat only fish we've caught ourselves. Drink too much whiskey — discuss art, religion, politics —

LADY EASTLAKE. Mr. Millais, you will miss your train. *(Blackout.)*

Scene 3

Lights up. A stage set with a few props to suggest the two-bedroom, thatched cottage of schoolmaster Alex Stewart, located by the Glenfinlas River in Brig o'Turk, Scotland. It is July 9, 1853. Crawley moves about the room unpacking trunks and suitcases, and putting things away.

RUSKIN. Yes, and all artists ever want to hear is how brilliant they are.

MILLAIS. God-like will do.

RUSKIN. Child-like, more to the point — spoiled children whose every brush stroke I am to praise.

MILLAIS. John, it's your power they resent.

RUSKIN. My power.

MILLAIS. You could have people believe a — a Titian would have been better employed painting cornflowers on china.

RUSKIN. Cornflowers. Simpletons.

MILLAIS. You could convince Titian himself.

RUSKIN. Can I convince you you're England's next Turner?

MILLAIS. It would be pleasant enough to let you try.

RUSKIN. Perhaps, I'll wait until I've seen my portrait.

MILLAIS. I have another idea for it!

RUSKIN. Another?

MILLAIS. There's a fantastic waterfall a short distance upriver from here. You standing on a crag before it. Do you see it? Your calm, placid figure in the foreground; the violent water coursing behind you.

RUSKIN. Hmm — how are you at painting cornflowers, Everett? *(Millais laughs.)*

MILLAIS. Tolerable enough. What's that you're writing?

RUSKIN. For my lectures. Listen, Everett. *(Reading from his notes.)* "Childish pride in knowledge was the first constituent element of the Renaissance."

MILLAIS. Oh, Mr. Ruskin, not our precious Renaissance.

RUSKIN. "Coldness and want of sympathy are written in Renaissance architecture as plainly as if they were graven on it in words. It is rigid, cold, inhuman."

MILLAIS. They will tear you limb from limb in Edinburgh.

RUSKIN. They will love each and every word. *(A woman comes from one of the two small bedrooms carrying clothes. She is about twenty-five and dressed in a simple, stylish way. She has thick auburn hair and is quite beautiful, though not conventionally so.)*

EFFIE. I think that will be all, Crawley.

CRAWLEY. Yes, ma'am.

EFFIE. Thank you.

RUSKIN. Effie, where did you pack the rest of my notes for the Edinburgh lectures?

EFFIE. In the box there, John, with the index for your book. *(Crawley leaves.)* I am so happy to have found this cottage. It's darling.

MILLAIS. Countess, your native Highland air has affected you most magically.

EFFIE. I beg your pardon?

MILLAIS. Indeed you might — installing your husband and myself — men of astounding, god-awful genius — in this chicken coop.

EFFIE. This chicken coop, Mr. Millais, will save you almost four pounds a week over the price of your hotel room. Even an artist need not starve if he practices a little economy.

RUSKIN. The advantages of a Scottish wife, Everett.

MILLAIS. But my room's no larger than a snuffbox. I can open the window, shut the door, and shave, all without getting out of bed. Such economy of movement, Countess. The Scots truly are geniuses of thrift.

EFFIE. God-awful geniuses, Mr. Millais.

RUSKIN. Wife, I think our friend would like something a bit more up-to-date, you know — paper-thin, with a Gothic gee-gaw or two.

EFFIE. No doubt.

MILLAIS. A real window in my room would suffice — not that little bit of business — more wood than glass.

RUSKIN. But, think, Everett, in such a room you are as a monk in his cell — and as the barest shade of light pervades the centuries-thick walls — you might commune with your deepest soul.

MILLAIS. Lord, the place depresses enough as it is.

RUSKIN. Admit it, Everett, it does have a certain rustic charm.

EFFIE. And Mrs. Stewart, our landlady, I'm told is a wonderful cook.

MILLAIS. Is she?

EFFIE. I thought that might interest you.

RUSKIN. Father will be pleased with the money we save.

MILLAIS. Oh, wherever you and the Countess are happy.

EFFIE. Good. It will be wonderful. Three months in a chicken coop with the Ruskins, Mr. Millais. Are you apprehensive?

MILLAIS. Not at all.

EFFIE. I should be, I hear the wife's mad.

RUSKIN. True enough.

EFFIE. You see.

MILLAIS. I just hear she's maddening.

EFFIE. You will see for yourself. Now, *(Picking up a pile of winter clothes.)* Mrs. Stewart said we might store our winter things with her until we need them. Have you anything for her, Mr. Millais?

MILLAIS. No.

EFFIE. Oh, and after all your complaints about the size of your room. *(Effie leaves. Ruskin casually takes a small book from the breast pocket of his jacket and makes a notation in it.)*

MILLAIS. John, your wife is an absolute delight. It is impossible to help liking her.

RUSKIN. I'm glad, Everett. *(Ruskin puts the small book back in his jacket.)* I hope you will always admire her.

MILLAIS. I'm certain I will.

RUSKIN. The certainty of a bachelor.

MILLAIS. Pardon me?

RUSKIN. I only mean, my dear Millais, there are no certainties where women are concerned.

MILLAIS. You speak in riddles, John.

RUSKIN. It's only I know how my wife appears to you because she appeared so once to me.

MILLAIS. She is not what she seems?

RUSKIN. She is just what she seems.

MILLAIS. More riddles.

RUSKIN. One last. How is it that all bachelors marry goddesses, but husbands live only with women? To answer that riddle, Everett, you must first marry.

MILLAIS. A goddess?

RUSKIN. A woman.

MILLAIS. *(Standing up and grabbing a sketchpad.)* No more of your riddles, John.

RUSKIN. Where are you going?

MILLAIS. The Glenfinlas to make some preliminary sketches for your portrait. *(Effie enters.)* Countess, I am off to sketch by the river. If I'm not back by dinner, please have old lady Stewart put aside something for me. I am especially fond of anything in the way of sweetbreads — that sort of thing. And please see what can be done to keep everything warm as possible, as I don't like cold food.

EFFIE. Indeed?

MILLAIS. Indeed. *(Millais leaves.)*

EFFIE. Amusing, isn't he?

RUSKIN. Very.

EFFIE. And spoiled, certainly. Early fame and London have seen to that. I like him though, he reminds me a bit of my brother George.

RUSKIN. Yes.

EFFIE. I'm so happy we're here.

RUSKIN. Lovely, isn't it?

EFFIE. And away from London.

RUSKIN. Is London such a trial for you, Effie?

EFFIE. No, only — *(Pause.)* We seem to get on so well, when we're away. *(Pause.)* Remember Venice, how happy we were?

RUSKIN. I was so proud of you.

EFFIE. Were you?

RUSKIN. Of course I was.

EFFIE. You never told me.

RUSKIN. Do you remember the Grand Duchess' ball? *(Pause.)* How ridiculous she looked. A whole jeweler's shop of diamonds shaken over her 'til she looked like a chandelier. *(Pause.)* And you — your green satin dress — the whiteness of your shoulders — eclipsing her. Everyone remarked it. Never have I seen anything more beautiful. Is it possible I never told you? *(Pause.)* I wish the world could always be Venice for you, Effie. But it can't.

EFFIE. Yes, I know.

RUSKIN. And, dear, you must know, it's not London that makes you so unhappy.

EFFIE. But, I feel there as if I would suffocate.

RUSKIN. With all your friends? My parents?

EFFIE. Yes, but —

RUSKIN. Where you are so loved and admired.

EFFIE. What matters that, if I don't know that you love me.

RUSKIN. Love you? Effie, I couldn't possibly love you more. No man could. *(Blackout.)*

Scene 4

Lights up. The schoolmaster's cottage. July 10, 1853. Ruskin and Millais are in the midst of a conversation.

RUSKIN. The problem, of course, being that you, Rossetti, and the rest know nothing of life.

MILLAIS. Yes, Father Ruskin.

RUSKIN. One day we will go to Lucca, and I'll show you della Quercia's sculpture of Ilaria di Caretto. You will not believe the perfect sweetness of her lips and closed eyes, or the way her dress folds closely beneath the curve of her breasts.

MILLAIS. Good Lord.

RUSKIN. Her hair — exquisite — like that of the Magdalene — its undulations just felt as it touches the softness of her cheek.

MILLAIS. I say a short note to the Countess, and on to Lucca, John.

RUSKIN. *(Smiling and shaking his head.)* As I said, nothing of life. *(Ruskin stands.)* Well, I have to see Alex Stewart. Then I think I'll go for a walk. I'll be back by tea. *(Ruskin takes a plaid from the coatrack and is about to leave; he turns back to Millais.)* I'm so glad you joined us, Everett.

MILLAIS. As am I, John. *(Ruskin leaves. Millais sits down on the sofa and begins to sketch. Effie walks in. She is carrying a bouquet of foxgloves. She sees Millais sketching, but says nothing in order not to disturb him. She looks into a small sideboard for a glass container to put the flowers in. She finds one and pours water into it from a pitcher. Millais looks up.)* Oh! Flowers now for our little heap of mud and thatch.

EFFIE. Are you to tease me all the while we're in Scotland, Mr. Millais? Haven't I brothers enough for that?

MILLAIS. No, Countess, you need one more at least. You're not sufficiently humble.

EFFIE. *(Arranging the flowers.)* One more or a thousand would make no difference. Ask my husband. *(She continues to cut, trim and arrange the foxgloves. Suddenly, she looks up.)* Where is John?

MILLAIS. To see Mr. Stewart, then for a walk. *(Pause.)* He said he'd be back for tea. Why? Is something wrong?

EFFIE. No.

MILLAIS. Are you sure?

EFFIE. *(Shortly.)* Yes, I've said so. *(Millais returns to his sketching, and there is an uncomfortable silence. Effie finishes arranging the flowers, then walks over and presents one of the foxgloves to Millais.)* From a short-tempered sister to her teasing brother.

MILLAIS. Thank you, Countess.

EFFIE. So now I have five brothers. How will I tell my mother?

MILLAIS. Countess, would you let me paint your portrait on one of the small canvases I have with me?

EFFIE. I'm flattered.

MILLAIS. Good. Yes. Now, I think I'd like you to be reading a book perhaps, or arranging flowers — I want you looking down at an angle in order to better emphasize your odd beauty.

EFFIE. My odd beauty? Might I be sewing? I'm making my little sister, Sophia, a dress and —

MILLAIS. Sewing. Perfect. Here, *(Quickly getting up and taking Effie by the hand, then grabbing a small chair by the window.)* now sit in this chair. Yes, the light is good. I'll make a quick sketch. *(He runs back to the sofa to get his sketch pad.)*

EFFIE. Mr. Millais, may I at least get my sewing?

MILLAIS. Of course — of course — but, be quick about it. *(Effie goes to her room. Millais looks excitedly around the parlor. His eyes rest on the foxgloves. He walks over and picks up the vase, then hands it quickly to Effie as she comes from her room with her sewing.)* Put these in your hair. *(Effie struggles a moment to balance the vase and her sewing.)*

EFFIE. A woman sewing with foxgloves in her hair?

MILLAIS. Oh, no one will notice you're sewing. They'll only see a beautiful woman — her lovely face framed in flowers — in deep contemplation. So many questions! *(Effie begins to arrange the flowers in her hair.)* No, none near the front. By the sides. Yes, very good. Yes. Yes. Excellent. Now sit down. *(Effie sits down. Millais grabs another chair, then sits down and begins to sketch.)* You may speak, but *do not*, under any circumstances, look up from your sewing.

EFFIE. How you toss and order one about; you are the most ridiculous man I have ever met.

MILLAIS. You inspire me. Don't move your head like that.

EFFIE. And like all artists, an utter despot.

MILLAIS. Please! *(Effie settles down to sewing. Millais, concentrating intently, sketches quickly. After several moments, he relaxes visibly, and begins to speak.)* Countess, may I ask a question? Why were you angry your husband left?

EFFIE. You will know, Mr. Millais, when you have a wife of your own.

MILLAIS. Apparently having a wife makes a man very wise. Your husband told me some riddles he said I would only understand once married.

EFFIE. Riddles?

MILLAIS. Something about bachelors marrying goddesses, but husbands living only with women.

EFFIE. How singular my husband's mind is. Perhaps he meant all bachelors ridiculous and husbands fortunate. I know he married a woman. Could he have wanted a goddess? What is a goddess, Mr. Millais?

MILLAIS. Countess, you're asking a bachelor. We know absolutely nothing. I don't even know why you were angry your husband left.

EFFIE. It embarrasses me to have to say this, but sometimes my husband forgets the finer points and leaves me alone in the company of men — or rather I should say — a man. He shouldn't.

MILLAIS. The absent-minded scholar.

EFFIE. Do you think so? Perhaps that's it. *(Millais nods.)* You are a good friend to my husband, Mr. Millais.

MILLAIS. I'll be indebted to him always for his letters to the *Times* when we were being attacked by the Royal Academy. The *(Scornfully.)* Royal Academy ... Sir Joshua Reynolds — Sir Sloshua!

EFFIE. Sir Sloshua, indeed. I like his work.

MILLAIS. And where have you seen human beings that look like his — skin that translucent and pure?

EFFIE. I think it lovely.

MILLAIS. Lovely! Besides, the man was a fool — shackling generations of Academy artists with that code.

EFFIE. You're being unfair. It was merely meant as a guideline —

MILLAIS. Artists don't need guidelines.

EFFIE. Not young ones certainly.

MILLAIS. One must have the eye of a draper to paint in such a fashion. Art! That's decoration. Art is Nature. Color. Light — light — and more light. It is beauty and blemish at once — the limpid eye *and* the pallid complexion, the —

EFFIE. Mr. Millais, you go too far with your Pre-Raphaelitism, and I insist in this portrait you minimize my nose — and by all means use as much light as you need to do so.

MILLAIS. Oh, the Academy would approve. How *pretty* you will look. But far less interesting, and incalculably less beautiful.

EFFIE. *(Perplexed and charmed.)* I hardly know what you mean. I'm speechless.

MILLAIS. Try to remain so. I'm drawing your mouth. *(Millais sketches quickly another moment, then speaks.)* To idealize is to destroy. Smother. We must always, as your husband said, go to Nature in all singleness of heart. *(Millais looks up from his sketching.)* Your expression a shade too somber — yes, better. *(Millais sketches another moment before speaking.)* Countess, your face has changed little since our first meeting.

EFFIE. Is two years so long a time?

MILLAIS. Two years! We met nearly eight years ago. At Ewell Castle — a dance. You don't remember?

EFFIE. I remember a dance at Ewell Castle. I don't remember you.

MILLAIS. Thank you, Countess.

EFFIE. Oh, I —

MILLAIS. No, please don't say anything, or I'll never get this right. *(Millais quickly sketches in silence before suddenly speaking again.)* Actually, I didn't expect you'd remember me. I asked my friends to introduce me to you — to the beautiful girl with the auburn hair. I was so nervous. You were so haughty.

EFFIE. Was I?

MILLAIS. Oh! Haughty and bored. I was only a boy, and grown men were fighting to dance with you. How scornful you were, Countess. Scornful and cruel to a wheezing, squeaky young boy. There now. *(Putting a final flourish to his sketch pad.)* Done.

EFFIE. Was I really so scornful and cruel?

MILLAIS. *(Looking up from his sketch pad, surprised at her tone.)* Not at all.

EFFIE. Thank you, Mr. Millais, but I think you spoke the truth first. I was so very proud. I wish I could speak to the boy you were then.

MILLAIS. Why? What would you say to him?

EFFIE. I would say, please forgive her. She is a vain, foolish, spoiled creature and no fate you might wish her could be worse than the one she will have to endure if she is ever to be anything better. *(Effie gets up slowly and walks over to the vase and starts to arrange the foxgloves in it. Millais looks at her thoughtfully a moment before speaking.)*

MILLAIS. It's true, you were proud, Countess, but even as a boy I could see what is ever more apparent to me now. That you had a kind and generous heart. *(Effie looks up at Millais when the door to the cottage opens and Ruskin walks in.)*

RUSKIN. It's begun to rain. *(Standing at the door and shaking his arms to throw off the water.)* I ran all the way back.

EFFIE. Here, John, give me your plaid. I'll lay it out to dry in my room.

RUSKIN. Yes, thank you. *(Ruskin gives Effie his plaid, and she takes it into her room.)* So, Everett, what have you sketched?

MILLAIS. *(Handing his sketch pad to Ruskin.)* The Countess.

RUSKIN. Mrs. Ruskin?

EFFIE. *(Appearing at the door to her room with her bonnet and jacket on.)* I'll have Crawley set out tea. Then, I must fly. I told Mrs. Stewart I would go into town with her, to help buy provisions for our stay.

MILLAIS. On a day like this?

EFFIE. In the Highlands, Mr. Millais, all days are like today. I'm afraid you may soon long for your warm, dry studio in Gower Street. *(Effie leaves.)*

RUSKIN. *(Looking at Millais' sketch of his wife.)* Everett, this is excellent. There's a kind of Oriental delicacy to it.

MILLAIS. Just a study. I'm going to make a painting, whilst I wait for your canvas to arrive from London.

RUSKIN. You've caught her expression exactly.

MILLAIS. Her manner, yes — but, something's missed — a certain melancholy, I think — *(Pause.)* Odd, that I should never have seen it before. *(Ruskin hesitates.)*

RUSKIN. Everett, we are to live in such a confined way these next few months, I —

MILLAIS. Yes, John?

RUSKIN. Everett, trusting in our friendship —

MILLAIS. What is it, John?

RUSKIN. Everett, my wife, though you could hardly have guessed it, suffers from fits of anger and deep depression.

MILLAIS. I can't imagine such a thing.

RUSKIN. I have been most apprehensive lest she speak sharply to you, or be uncivil in some way. I knew you could not possibly understand.

MILLAIS. I see.

RUSKIN. What is it, Everett?

MILLAIS. Nothing really — only before, when the Countess found you had gone and left us alone, she became, I thought, unusually agitated.

RUSKIN. Mrs. Ruskin is convinced I leave her alone with certain men to compromise her.

MILLAIS. What?

RUSKIN. It is a morbid notion, which possesses her, and nothing I can do or say will convince her otherwise.

MILLAIS. I'm sorry, John.

RUSKIN. Please, Everett, I don't mean to upset you, and I am quite hopeful as she has promised to see a physician on our return if she feels no better.

MILLAIS. Poor thing. Such a surprise. I suppose one never truly knows another human being.

RUSKIN. No. Never. (*Blackout.*)

Scene 5

Lights up. The schoolmaster's cottage. Mid-August 1853. Everett Millais enters. He walks over to a table and picks up a sketch pad and begins to look through it. Effie comes from her room.

MILLAIS. Your sketching has improved markedly since our last lesson.

EFFIE. Do you think so?

MILLAIS. Very much.

EFFIE. Mr. Millais, your thumb. It's bleeding!

MILLAIS. Oh. *(Millais tries to hide his thumb.)* So it is. Yes.

EFFIE. What happened? Let me see. *(Effie examines Millais' thumb.)*

MILLAIS. I was making a bridge of stones across the river — the shallow end — when one of the stones slipped.

EFFIE. Oh dear, let me get something to stop the bleeding. *(Effie goes to a drawer, finds a piece of cloth, and begins to bandage Millais' thumb.)* A bridge?

MILLAIS. That it might be easier to get into town.

EFFIE. Such a lot of bother, when all you and John have to do is to take off your shoes, roll up your trousers, and —

MILLAIS. But you're forever having to walk the long way 'round.

EFFIE. Oh. *(Pause.)* How kind of you to notice.

MILLAIS. It's nothing.

EFFIE. Certainly it is. Thank you, Mr. Millais. *(Millais continues to look through the sketch pad.)*

MILLAIS. This rock formation — superb. *(He turns to the next page.)* John and I fishing in the Glenfinlas. I didn't know you were there that day.

EFFIE. On a hill further upstream sketching, when I saw the two of you. I hope you don't mind.

MILLAIS. Of course not. You've caught John's manner exactly — mine, too, for all I know. Very good. I'd know that was John anywhere. *(Pause.)* He's very different, isn't he? I thought I knew him, but I don't — it's impossible — his soul is always in the clouds and out of reach of ordinary mortals. *(Millais waits for a moment for a response from Effie, but she says nothing.)* I'm sorry. I don't mean to speak to you so freely about your husband, it's just that — oh, never mind. Countess, this is excellent. If I had to make one criticism it would be —

EFFIE. My roses. Crimes against Nature.

MILLAIS. Oh, but —

EFFIE. Please. Don't try to spare my feelings.

MILLAIS. But, they're so easy. Someone with your ability should have no difficulty with them. Perhaps, *(Picking up a pencil.)* if you held your pencil at more of an angle like this. Several *(He begins to draw.)* strokes this way, one or two that, two more strokes here. Very simple. A line here and there, a bit of shading — some definition — and — there — you — are — a little rough perhaps — but a standard rose. Try it.

EFFIE. *(Taking the pencil.)* Oh dear, my rose looks like one of Mrs. Stewart's scones next to yours. How unfortunate — how lumpy it looks. It's a currant scone, I believe. Like *(She looks to Millais, to make sure she is holding the pencil as suggested.)* this? *(Millais nods. Effie begins to draw. Millais watches over her shoulder.)*

MILLAIS. Good. Very good. Far less scone-like.

EFFIE. Yes, rather more like a tea cake.

MILLAIS. You mustn't get discouraged.

EFFIE. Discouraged? I'm getting hungry. *(They laugh. Effie continues to draw as Millais watches her. He speaks suddenly.)*

MILLAIS. Well. I really must be getting back.

EFFIE. Oh, of course. I didn't mean to keep you.

MILLAIS. No. Not at all. Please — please continue with your drawing. *(Ruskin walks in.)*

RUSKIN. How does your pupil get on?

MILLAIS. Beautifully.

RUSKIN. *(Looking at Millais' bandaged thumb.)* This sketching is dangerous business.

MILLAIS. A little accident. But your wife has made me good as new. Now I must go, if I'm ever to finish my work. *(Millais leaves.)*

RUSKIN. What a boy he is.

EFFIE. John, I — might we move back to the hotel?

RUSKIN. The hotel?

EFFIE. This cottage is, I fear, too confining.

RUSKIN. But it was you who chose it. *(Pause.)* Effie, what's troubling you? *(Effie does not respond.)* Effie, when I looked for my diary yesterday, I found it had been moved. *(Effie is silent.)* Had you asked me, I'd have given it to you.

EFFIE. I don't want it.

RUSKIN. Then why did you take it?

EFFIE. I thought to burn it.

RUSKIN. Burn it? Why, Effie? *(Effie does not respond.)* And were I to let you burn it, would that make you well? Then burn it, Effie. I would little miss it. *(Blackout.)*

Scene 6

Lights up. Mid-September 1853. The schoolmaster's cottage. Everett Millais is sitting on a sofa reading a book. John Ruskin is seated at a dining table writing. Effie Ruskin is sketching.

EFFIE. Mr. Millais, I had a thought ... about your belief in absolute fidelity to Nature.

MILLAIS. I should never have given you so much as a single lesson.

EFFIE. You decide to paint a tree. When exactly would you paint it? Spring? Winter? Surely a different tree each time.

RUSKIN. Effie, Everett is —

MILLAIS. I would paint it at a single moment. In the spring. Each blossom. The winter. The naked beauty of every branch.

EFFIE. But, might not there be more of craftsmanship than —

RUSKIN. Effie, in the Pre-Raphaelites lays the foundation of a school of art nobler than the world has seen for three hundred years, but you would ask Millais —

MILLAIS. It's all right, John.

EFFIE. My thought is this — after seeing a Turner — one never again looks at the sea in quite the same way. Now, surely that cannot be because he has painted it as we might see it ourselves from any beach.

MILLAIS. Yes, Countess, but might it not be as powerful to capture in an instant — *(Effie puts down her sketching.)*

EFFIE. Pray, if you would save your reply just a moment, Mr. Millais. Now, I am going to insist the two of you stop what you

30

are doing immediately and come with me for a walk. That we would sit in on such a day —

RUSKIN. Not now, Effie.

EFFIE. But, John, it is absolutely glorious out, and you never —

RUSKIN. *(Very angrily.)* Not now.

EFFIE. I was unaware we were dispensing with even the most basic forms of civility.

RUSKIN. Don't you realise how important these lectures are to my career? *(Pause.)* Indeed, Effie, your sole purpose of late seems to be to annoy and distract me to such an extent that I am incapable of doing my work. *(Effie smiles awkwardly at Millais, then turns quickly and leaves. Ruskin goes back to his writing. Millais returns to his reading. A moment later, Ruskin looks over at Millais, and seeing that he is reading, reaches into the breast pocket of his jacket for the small book he keeps there. He takes it out and begins to write in it. Millais looks up from his book and observes Ruskin, but resumes reading just as Ruskin closes the small book and puts it back in his jacket. Ruskin waits a moment, then addresses Millais.)* I'm sorry, Everett, I suppose you think me rather too severe with my wife. *(Millais looks up from his book, but doesn't say anything.)* But, you must understand. There are times she needs to be handled firmly, or she is capable of — I don't know what one might call it — an excess of feeling, I suppose. *(Millais still does not respond.)* Oh, I can't make you see.

MILLAIS. No, John, I'm beginning to see.

RUSKIN. Are you?

MILLAIS. Yes.

RUSKIN. Good. Then, perhaps you can help her.

MILLAIS. If I can help the Countess in any way, I will.

RUSKIN. The Countess. Why is it you insist on calling *my wife* the Countess?

MILLAIS. I don't know. I suppose because it suits her.

RUSKIN. Because she is proud?

MILLAIS. Because there is a dignity about her. Because she has grace, wit, and intelligence. Because —

RUSKIN. I see you have given it some thought. *(Millais is silent.)* At all events, Everett, sometimes after so many years, grace, wit, and intelligence can seem more like high self-regard,

31

sarcasm, and arrogance.

MILLAIS. Truly?

RUSKIN. Truly. *(Pause.)* As for my wife — you think her lovely now? You should have known her when she was a child. Eleven. Twelve years old. What a beauty she was. Innocent. Fascinating. Pure.

MILLAIS. Are you really comparing the girl to the woman in this fashion and finding the woman wanting?

RUSKIN. I only —

MILLAIS. I should as soon look to an acorn for shade and shun the sheltering arms of a great oak.

RUSKIN. If I seem harsh, it is only because I know what Mrs. Ruskin was. What she might be. If I hold women to a higher standard, it is only because my respect and admiration for their sex is equally high. I believe a woman should —

MILLAIS. Women, like men, are creatures of Nature, John, and Nature knows nothing of your higher standard. Nature must be our only teacher. You taught me that.

RUSKIN. Oh, I see. And now you are to be my teacher. Well, here then, *(Holding his pen out to Millais.)* Everett, you write my essays.

MILLAIS. They are already written, John. You need only read them. *(Ruskin returns to his writing, Millais to his book. Effie enters and turns towards her room. Ruskin speaks.)*

RUSKIN. Effie, I'd like you to finish gilding the illustrations for the Edinburgh lectures.

EFFIE. No, John, I don't think I will. *(Effie enters her room and closes the door. Ruskin looks at the closed door a moment, then turns and reaches into the inside pocket of his jacket for the small book. Doing so, he notices Millais watching him. The two men stare at each other a moment. Ruskin finally takes his hand from his jacket without retrieving the book, and returns to his writing. Millais stands and walks out of the cottage. Ruskin continues with his writing. Finally, he stops. He looks over to where Millais was sitting, then to Effie's closed door. He gets up and walks over to Effie's door. He stands outside it a moment, but turns finally away and resumes writing. Blackout.)*

Scene 7

Lights up. Late October 1853. The schoolmaster's cottage. Three months after the arrival of the Ruskins and Millais at Brig o'Turk. Effie Ruskin is seated on the sofa, writing a letter. It is late in the afternoon. Outside the rain is falling heavily and the light is beginning to fade. Everett Millais enters carrying a canvas with a cover to protect it. He is wearing a dense, heavy wool plaid blanket wrapped around his head and thrown over his shoulders.

EFFIE. Oh, let me help you with that. *(She goes to Millais and holds the canvas for him while he unwraps the plaid from his body and hangs it on a coatrack by the door to dry.)*
MILLAIS. *(Taking the canvas from her.)* Thank you, Countess. *(Millais takes the canvas and puts it in his room. Effie sits down again on the sofa. Millais reenters the room and sits in a nearby chair. He sees Effie's letter.)* I'm sorry, you were writing, please don't let me disturb you.
EFFIE. It's quite all right. It's a letter to my friend, Lady Eastlake, and I write as I speak to her, with long pauses between thoughts. Mr. Millais, is something wrong? You look so discouraged.
MILLAIS. It's nothing really. I don't know why it affects me so. I dropped my paint box and now find it broken beyond any hope of repair. Only an accident, but a melancholy one that has finished today's work.
EFFIE. I'm sorry.
MILLAIS. It's of no consequence. I do wish it would stop raining though, or we shall all go mad from this damp, or kill ourselves from the intense cold.
EFFIE. We will be home soon — only two more weeks — think on that.
MILLAIS. Yes.

33

EFFIE. Let me make you some tea, or perhaps some broth. I'm sure —

MILLAIS. *(Sharply.)* I don't want anything at the moment, thank you. *(Pause.)* I'm sorry, Countess. There's something weighing heavily on my mind right now, and it's driving me a little mad.

EFFIE. Is it something I can help you with?

MILLAIS. No. *(They are quiet a moment. Effie finally speaks.)*

EFFIE. How is my husband's portrait progressing?

MILLAIS. Not well. You know that little tent I rigged up so that I could paint in the rain? *(Effie nods.)* Well, I don't stay in the least dry, but the tent serves as a marvelous tube for the wind to drive through, quite chafing the back of my neck. And the stove I fashioned to keep out the chill produces a smothering smoke, not in the least warming but excessively unpleasant. I have chosen the wrong profession; I should be an architect. *(Pause.)* Countess, do you ever feel there's something depressing about the far-stretching mountains and mists hereabout; that at times the landscape is so wild and melancholy you can't help feeling so far away from everything you love — a feeling of complete despair?

EFFIE. Yes, of course.

MILLAIS. That's the way I was feeling a moment ago, but you have shaken me of it.

EFFIE. You flatter me, Mr. Millais, and if ever you feel my foolish talk and annoying ways can —

MILLAIS. I don't know anyone whose talk and ways are less foolish and annoying. And, it's not just that. Sometimes all I have to do is think about you and I feel at peace. *(Effie looks down.)* I'm sorry. I don't know why I go on this way. Perhaps it's because we are to leave soon, and London is so large, who knows how often we will meet there? I suppose I wanted you to know before we leave, something of my high regard for you. But, I see I have embarrassed you. I should keep silent about my feelings — they are childish, and —

EFFIE. Please don't say such a thing. I will always remember what you have just said. Please don't try to diminish it.

MILLAIS. Very well. Might I ask something of you then? Oh,

no. No — it's quite foolish.

EFFIE. No, please, what is it?

MILLAIS. Would you speak my name — my Christian name — once before we leave?

EFFIE. Your name?

MILLAIS. Yes.

EFFIE. Everett. *(Pause.)* I will miss you, Everett.

MILLAIS. Not more than I will miss you, Effie. *(Pause.)*

EFFIE. Where can Crawley be? He was to have —

MILLAIS. Did you know your friend Charlotte Ker told me that when she visited you in Venice, you created quite a sensation by commandeering a gondola and piloting it down the Grand Canal?

EFFIE. A sensation? I hardly think so. Charlotte! *(Pause.)* Although you should have seen the faces on all the people as our gondola slid past. They were appalled. Horrified! I tried so desperately to look serious.

MILLAIS. You wanted to laugh?

EFFIE. Laugh — no — I was ecstatic. The Grand Canal. A glorious day. The wind in my face, through my hair, billowing out my dress. It was thrilling. Absolutely thrilling.

MILLAIS. You must have looked magnificent.

EFFIE. Oh — no. At least my father-in-law didn't think so. As soon as he heard about it in London, he wrote John that he shrank from the thought of seeing the loveliest part of nature — by which of course he meant all womankind — unsex itself on the Grand Canal. *(Millais laughs.)* Yes. Yes, he did. My father, on the other hand, simply wrote to say when I was next home, I must see how long it would take me to row from Perth to Dundee on the River Tay. *(They both laugh.)*

MILLAIS. Are you looking forward to returning to London?

EFFIE. No, Scotland is my home and the country even in this weather is delightful to me.

MILLAIS. Is it really?

EFFIE. I'm so happy to be able to dash into the woods and down to the trout streams, without a bonnet. Or walk across the moors to a mountain lake, and sit quietly there and watch a great flock of seagulls flying.

MILLAIS. Strange. I think a crowded London drawing room at about eight or so in the evening as your natural setting. Not bonnetless amidst a swarm of seagulls.

EFFIE. In London I'm merely a ghost, haunting drawing rooms and theatres in search of an earthly life.

MILLAIS. But, it seems as if you were made for society.

EFFIE. I'm a clever ghost.

MILLAIS. A spectral genius.

EFFIE. *(Smiling.)* You are not a gentleman, Mr. Millais. You should accept my presentation of myself as a simple country-woman without comment. And it's true, I do love to be with people and to go to the theatre and dance, but —

MILLAIS. Yes. *(Pause.)* Please, what is it you were going to say?

EFFIE. I — I'm not sure.

MILLAIS. Try.

EFFIE. I suppose that there's a kind of compulsiveness to my behaviour in London that frightens me. I'm like a person who gorges on rich food without thought or pleasure and still knows nothing but hunger. Sometimes I think if I could only find a room more ablaze with light and people, or wear a more exquisite gown, then, perhaps, I wouldn't feel the way I do.

MILLAIS. And what way is that?

EFFIE. What way is that? *(She thinks for a long moment.)* Empty — empty. *(Pause.)* How I used to scorn such women — like the woman I've become, but I know — *(Effie hesitates, but continues.)* I know too well what I have lost in this world to care for the happiness other women have in trifles when they have lost the substance.

MILLAIS. What have you lost? *(Effie doesn't respond.)* Why are you so unhappy?

EFFIE. If ever I were to unburden myself to anyone, it would be you, Mr. Millais. How could anyone live close to you as we have done and not see how deeply the threads of kindness and decency are entwined in your nature. I cannot. *(Millais is quiet a long moment. He speaks suddenly.)*

MILLAIS. What is it your husband writes in that little book of his?

EFFIE. *(Taken aback.)* Things. Various things.

MILLAIS. What sort of things? *(Effie makes no attempt to respond.)* I think you know. I think he writes down bits and pieces of your conversation, criticisms of your dress, voice, and manner. And do you know what else I think? I think it a most unmanly and debased proceeding to spy and connive in such a way against one's wife, and to what end I can scarcely guess.

EFFIE. That later he might discuss — *(Pause.)* Mr. Millais, I confide in you despite myself.

MILLAIS. If only you would. If only I could help lighten this mysterious burden of yours.

EFFIE. Is it so obvious then?

MILLAIS. You hide it well with your lively ways, but sometimes behind your eyes or at the corners of your mouth a painful shadow lingers. I could paint forever and not convey hopelessness with the eloquence of that shadow.

EFFIE. Oh dear. Not hopeless, Mr. Millais. Your Countess sounds grim indeed. *(Millais stares at Effie sympathetically, but says nothing. She looks at him a moment, then speaks suddenly in a tone of profound desperation.)* I would run away if I could. I envy the people sweeping the crossings.

MILLAIS. Please let me help you.

EFFIE. No! What can you be thinking? Becoming entangled in my affairs would damage you irreparably.

MILLAIS. I don't care. I can't bear to see the way he treats you. Such a brilliant man. Such an eloquent lover of all things beautiful. Forever theorizing about God and the universe, then looking at a lovely woman in practical contempt. I think him nothing better than a quiet scoundrel.

EFFIE. Mr. Millais, he is my husband.

MILLAIS. I don't care.

EFFIE. But, I must!

MILLAIS. Very well. I'm sorry then. I'll leave before I say more. *(Millais walks to the door but stops before opening it.)* Forgive me, Countess. I don't know what compels me. Since we have been in Scotland a weight has been added to a scale that before lingered in perfect balance. Everything is altered now, and I feel half mad all the time. *(Millais leaves. Blackout.)*

Scene 8

Lights up. The schoolmaster's cottage one hour later. Ruskin enters. He quietly hangs up his plaid before speaking.

RUSKIN. Effie, I have to ride over to see Mr. MacNaughton. Where is Crawley?

EFFIE. I don't know.

RUSKIN. But he was to have met me here. Oh, he probably went directly to the hotel. Is Millais about?

EFFIE. No.

RUSKIN. Not back yet? I passed him on the road into town over an hour ago, without any covering from the rain, insisting he was going to get his hair cut at the hotel. I tried to tell him no one would be there, but he wouldn't listen, refusing even to come back for his plaid. I believe this dismal Scottish weather is oppressing him horribly.

EFFIE. He was rather discouraged this afternoon.

RUSKIN. Discouraged? I never knew such a miserable creature. He paints 'til his limbs are numb and his back has as many aches as joints in it. Either excited or depressed, always restless and unhappy.

EFFIE. John, he —

RUSKIN. Yes?

EFFIE. John, I think he has feelings for me.

RUSKIN. Do you?

EFFIE. I think he may be in love with me.

RUSKIN. Has he told you so?

EFFIE. No.

RUSKIN. Then how do you know?

EFFIE. I feel it.

RUSKIN. You feel it. Well, you may be right. No wonder Cupid is represented as a mischievous child when love makes such a fool

38

of a man.

EFFIE. John. *(Ruskin turns away from her, as if he had not heard her.)* John.

RUSKIN. Effie, don't start with this now. I'm late.

EFFIE. John, please don't go. I'm frightened.

RUSKIN. You're mad.

EFFIE. *(Taking Ruskin's hand.)* John.

RUSKIN. Let go of me. *(Effie kisses Ruskin passionately, pressing his hand against her breasts. Ruskin pushes her away.)* And that Millais might chance in at any moment is as nothing I suppose? *(Pause.)* My God, you may yet end up in Bedlam.

EFFIE. Why, John? *(Ruskin is silent.)* You loved me once. What of the letters — all the letters filled with passion and longing for me? *(Ruskin makes no attempt to respond.)* John, what's wrong with me!

RUSKIN. Do you really want me to go over it all again?

EFFIE. No.

RUSKIN. For the last time, Effie, you are not what I think a woman should be.

EFFIE. No — no, I am not.

RUSKIN. No. A woman should be proud, beautiful, and noble like —

EFFIE. — like the de Milo Venus or a Florentine painting.

RUSKIN. As usual, you are being perverse.

EFFIE. You once thought that I was proud and beautiful.

RUSKIN. Yes, once.

EFFIE. And are you so disappointed to find I am only human after all?

RUSKIN. Only disappointed to find that you are insolent and willful.

EFFIE. Disappointed to find that I am insolent and willful?

RUSKIN. Yes.

EFFIE. *(Lashing out suddenly.)* No, John, disappointed to find that I am only a woman, not a smooth, white piece of marble or a luminous painting. Only a woman after all, with a fallible heart and weak human flesh!

RUSKIN. Calm yourself, and at once, Effie. I will not tolerate one of your fits now.

EFFIE. You! You've taken your love of beauty and turned it into something base and ugly and vicious.

RUSKIN. Who are you to speak to me in such a way?

EFFIE. You can't tolerate anything that won't yield to some absolute maxim of yours. You want the ideal. Not a woman, but a waxwork figure of one.

RUSKIN. I won't have this.

EFFIE. Always beautiful, never in pain, never in need or needed by you.

RUSKIN. Don't you dare.

EFFIE. You don't want anything that is strange or spontaneous, or that doesn't look, sound or move exactly the way you think it should.

RUSKIN. *(Grabbing her fiercely.)* Like you?

EFFIE. John.

RUSKIN. I don't like the way you look, sound, or move. You have a beautiful face, but your person is not formed to excite passion. In fact there are — as we both know — certain circumstances in your person which completely check it.

EFFIE. Stop, John. Please stop.

RUSKIN. Frankly, I had always imagined women quite different from what I saw you were. Then to find —

EFFIE. Please don't say anymore. Please.

RUSKIN. Why do you do force me to this? *(Pause.)* Effie, I don't think we need discuss this again. When we married, I expected to change you; you expected to change me. Neither has succeeded and both are displeased. It is the same with Millais. When we came to Scotland I expected to do great things for him. I saw he was proud and impatient, and thought to make him meek and methodical. I might as well have tried to make a Highland stream meek and methodical. Come now, Effie, collect yourself. Remember I have always admired you for your dignity. What just happened was — well, we will forget all about it and carry on. Now, Crawley was supposed to meet me here fifteen min — *(Millais enters. Effie quickly brushes the corners of her eyes.)* Everett, soaked through for all your trouble, and no haircut. I tried to tell you it was too late.

MILLAIS. I wasn't thinking — I'll go tomorrow. Pardon me, I must change my shirt. *(Millais goes to his room. Ruskin calls to him.)*

RUSKIN. Everett, if you like, Mrs. Ruskin will cut your hair. *(Effie looks up slowly and stares at her husband in disbelief.)* Yes, she cuts her brothers' hair, her father's, mine as well. She's an excellent barber. Quite an artist really.

MILLAIS. *(Coming to the door of his room buttoning his shirt and looking towards Effie.)* No, I couldn't. Really I —

RUSKIN. Nonsense. We won't hear of it. She's better than any barber. When I get back, I expect to see you looking trim and spiffy as a rich country parson. *(He walks towards the door and opens it.)* Effie, if Crawley shows up here, send him at once to meet me at the hotel. I've hired two horses to take us to the MacNaughtons'. *(Ruskin waits a moment for Effie to acknowledge his request. When she does not, he turns and leaves. Millais stands quietly in the doorway to his room. Effie sits on the sofa with her face turned away from him. After a long moment of awkward silence, Millais speaks.)*

MILLAIS. You don't have to cut my hair. It can wait.

EFFIE. No, I'll cut it.

MILLAIS. It's not necessary.

EFFIE. *(Getting up and walking over to the sideboard and looking through a drawer there for scissors and a comb.)* I don't mind. Really.

MILLAIS. Very well. *(He walks over and sits in a chair.)*

EFFIE. *(Taking a towel from the cupboard.)* Perhaps it would be better if you sat on the trunk there, Mr. Millais. You are taller than any of my brothers.

MILLAIS. Oh, yes, of course. *(He takes a small trunk by the side of the cupboard and places it in the center of the room and sits down.)*

EFFIE. *(Picks up newspaper from a table by the sofa and lays it out on the chair Millais has just vacated. She turns to him and lays the towel very tentatively on the back of his shoulders.)* If you would just hold that 'round your neck.

MILLAIS. All right ... yes. *(Effie picks up the comb and stands behind Millais. She hesitates, then finally runs the comb slowly through his hair, combing it back away from his forehead. She puts the comb down and picks up the scissors. She reaches up, falters, then reaches up again and takes his hair in her hand. She cuts off a small piece, which she lays down on the open newspaper. She cuts off several more pieces, then circles 'round in front of Millais. She gently lifts his head by placing the tips of her fingers beneath his chin. She looks into his face, then slowly backs away from him, silently putting the scissors down. Millais takes hold of her dress and squeezes it tightly in his hand.)* Effie.

EFFIE. Mr. Millais, I —

MILLAIS. Effie. *(Effie looks down and shakes her head.)* Effie. *(He gets up and stands behind her.)* Effie, I love you. I love you so that I'm sick with it. Effie, *(He moves closer to her.)* when I'm near you, I swear I feel the breath of God upon me. *(He puts his arm around her waist. She turns towards him and he kisses her passionately. She pulls herself away and walks to the other side of the room.)* I suppose I should say I'm sorry, but I'm not. I can't bear it any longer. Can't bear to see you every day and not hold you. Can't bear to see the way he mistreats and neglects you — squanders what I would give all I have for the scantest portion of.

EFFIE. Please, if you have any mercy, I beg you, not another word!

MILLAIS. But, I —

EFFIE. I beg you! *(Millais is about to speak. Effie, desperately:)* Please! *(Millais looks at Effie for some time before speaking.)*

MILLAIS. I'm sorry. *(Millais turns and walks into his room. A moment later he comes out carrying a satchel.)* I'm going to move back to the hotel. I'll send for the rest of my things tomorrow. *(Millais turns and walks towards the door. He turns back to Effie.)* Effie. *(Pause.)* Effie, I'm sorry for speaking, when I should have kept silent. Please know the words did not come cheaply, I will pay dearly for them through all the days of my life without you. *(Pause.)* Goodbye. *(Millais turns to leave. Ruskin walks in.)*

RUSKIN. *(Angrily.)* Where is Crawley? I've been waiting for — what is this? Millais, where are you going?

MILLAIS. I've decided to move back to the hotel. I fear I have a sudden craving for solitude.

RUSKIN. Oh? All right then. Can I help you with your things?

MILLAIS. No. Thank you. I'll send someone 'round for them tomorrow. *(Millais leaves.)*

RUSKIN. I suppose it would be useless to remind him he has once again forgotten his plaid. And what has happened to our young genius that he feels compelled to bolt in the night?

EFFIE. What do you think happened, John?

RUSKIN. I haven't a clue.

EFFIE. I think you have, John. I told you Millais was in love with me. Why did you leave me alone with him? Why did you tell him I would cut his hair? What did you think would happen?

RUSKIN. I thought that whatever happened, you were my wife and I could trust you.

EFFIE. Damn you.

RUSKIN. Madam, you forget yourself.

EFFIE. If only I could, John. Forget myself, my parents, my brothers and sisters, my position — my duty before God. Forget everything! I would. And I would go to Everett Millais and tell him that I love him. Love his mind, his soul, and his body.

RUSKIN. I have never heard a woman speak in such a way. You are what my father always said you were, lowborn and lowbred.

EFFIE. And you, John Ruskin, mild, forbearing author of psalms to art and beauty. I defy you. I curse you. And if ever I were to suffer the pains of eternal torment, they could be no worse to me than going home to London with you, and I will not go. *(Blackout.)*

End of Act One

ENTR'ACTE

1ST VOICE. The Queen cannot, despite her great fondness for your father, grant his request.

2ND VOICE. Did Her Majesty ever once look to the facts?

1ST VOICE. Her Majesty feels that were she to receive your mother back into society, it might be seen as in some way sanctioning your mother's behaviour.

2ND VOICE. Behaviour!

1ST VOICE. I'm sorry.

2ND VOICE. No. Father asks that this letter be put before Her Majesty. In it every particular of the case has been —

1ST VOICE. But, this is futile.

2ND VOICE. He insists.

ACT TWO

Scene 1

Lights up. A stage set with a few props to suggest the Philosophical Institution at Edinburgh. November 1853. Sound effects to suggest over a thousand enthusiastic listeners. Ruskin is center stage.

RUSKIN. I say, therefore, that the greatest art is that which conveys to the mind of the beholder — by any means whatsoever — the greatest number of the greatest ideas — and allows him to *see*. *(Pause.)* For the greatest thing a human soul ever does in this world is to *see*. Hundreds can talk for one who can think, but thousands can think for one who can see. To see clearly is poetry, prophecy, and religion all in one. *(Pause.)* And where the Renaissance erred was in the setting of Beauty above Truth, and seeking for it always at the expense of truth. The proper punishment of such pursuit — the punishment which all the laws of the universe render inevitable — is that those who thus pursue beauty should wholly lose sight of it. *(Applause.)* For Truth — the truth of Nature is part of the truth of God; to him who does not search it out, darkness, as to him that does, infinity. *(Wild Applause. Blackout.)*

Scene 2

Lights up. December 1853. London. The drawing room at Denmark Hill. Effie is sketching. Mrs. Ruskin enters.

MRS. RUSKIN. Effie, why did you rush in such a way from the dinner table? *(Effie is silent. Mrs. Ruskin sits down. She waits a moment, then speaks.)* Effie, dear, Mr. Ruskin, John, and I are all very distressed for you. John most especially.
EFFIE. Is he?
MRS. RUSKIN. Effie, this is hardly the time for impertinence. *(Pause.)* And despite what you may believe, our one wish is to see you truly well again. *(Pause.)* Now, dear, there is a doctor in Hampstead who specialises in nervous disorders. We would like you to see him. You needn't be frightened. I will make every arrangement, and accompany you so that —
EFFIE. No.
MRS. RUSKIN. Effie, I —
EFFIE. No.
MRS. RUSKIN. Very well, Effie. Under the circumstances, I think I must write your mother.
EFFIE. I respectfully ask that you do not.
MRS. RUSKIN. You will see the doctor then?
EFFIE. To what end? That I might tell him that you will be kind

to me, but only so long as I praise you as three perfect people and never once complain?

MRS. RUSKIN. Euphemia. *(Effie is silent.)* I will forgive this outburst because you are ill. *(Mr. Ruskin enters the room. Mrs. Ruskin goes to him and speaks confidentially.)* She will not go.

MR. RUSKIN. As I expected.

MRS. RUSKIN. What are we to do, Mr. Ruskin? I fear for her as I never have before.

MR. RUSKIN. I know, Mrs. Ruskin.

MRS. RUSKIN. This is so very painful.

MR. RUSKIN. Unhappy child.

MRS. RUSKIN. I suppose the Lord has given us this burden, that we might divine His lesson in it for us. *(Crawley enters carrying a tray with a decanter and four glasses on it.)*

MR. RUSKIN. On the table there, Crawley. Thank you. *(Ruskin enters. Crawley leaves. Mrs. Ruskin looks at her son and shakes her head. Effie rises.)*

EFFIE. John, I wish to speak with you.

RUSKIN. Yes.

EFFIE. Privately.

MR. RUSKIN. Effie, whatever it is you have to say to John, I'm sure we might all profit from.

EFFIE. John, I wish to speak with you alone.

MRS. RUSKIN. Effie, we are a family. If there is something in particular ...

EFFIE. John. *(Ruskin does not respond.)* Please. *(Ruskin still does not respond. Effie walks out of the room.)*

MRS. RUSKIN. If that girl is not mad, she is the boldest creature I ever knew.

MR. RUSKIN. John. John. I want to speak to you. Now! I never saw the like. *(Mr. Ruskin pours three glasses of port, taking one, and giving one to his wife and one to his son.)*

RUSKIN. She probably only wanted to know why I hadn't discussed the doctor with her myself.

MR. RUSKIN. You will not excuse her, John. You do her no good, despite what you intend.

RUSKIN. Since Scotland, she has been every day less well.

MRS. RUSKIN. It has not affected her sketching.

MR. RUSKIN. Would the same could be said for her conduct.

RUSKIN. Of course, no one will ever believe her conduct to be what it is.

MRS. RUSKIN. And no one, as we have latterly seen, can be ruder than that girl when she has a mind to.

RUSKIN. Millais thought her perfection.

MR. RUSKIN. I have no doubt.

RUSKIN. Would that he had been with her yesterday at tea.

MRS. RUSKIN. At tea?

RUSKIN. That he might have heard her refer to her husband — his father and his mother as "that Batch of Ruskins."

MRS. RUSKIN. Batch of Ruskins!

RUSKIN. Delivered with a snap and a toss of her head before flying from the table.

MR. RUSKIN. That girl will starve to death if she continues so.

MRS. RUSKIN. Father.

RUSKIN. We should never have gone to Scotland.

MR. RUSKIN. I told you it was wrongheaded of you, John.

RUSKIN. I know, Father. I realised it the day we arrived.

MR. RUSKIN. John?

RUSKIN. Perhaps, if I read it for you.

MRS. RUSKIN. Calmly, John. *(Ruskin takes his book from his jacket and searches through it.)*

RUSKIN. Here. Scotland. The day of our arrival. *(Ruskin begins to read from his book.)*

"Millais and John are having a lively discussion."

(Ruskin looks up from his book.) Art and so on.

"Effie suddenly insinuates herself into their conversation.

Effie: Three months cooped up — "

(Ruskin looks up from his book.) Cooped up!

MR. RUSKIN. Charming.

RUSKIN. " — with the Ruskins, Mr. Millais. You must be extremely apprehensive.

Millais: — looks to John, embarrassed, and tries to make light of it — Why no. Of course not.

Effie: You should be. *They* say his wife is mad."

MRS. RUSKIN. They?

RUSKIN. Her meaning was clear. We, of course.

MRS. RUSKIN. Oh, dear.

MR. RUSKIN. Recompense, I presume, for all our worry about her.

MRS. RUSKIN. John, she embarrasses only herself. *(Mr. Ruskin refills his glass and his wife's. Ruskin shakes his head "no" when his father offers him more port.)*

RUSKIN. Embarrass? *(Putting the small book back into the breast pocket of his jacket.)* Effie? It's as nothing to her. She has been indulged in all her wishes from her youth and feels any restraint whatsoever now an insult to her person. And her friend, Lady Eastlake, I believe —

MRS. RUSKIN. Don't mention that woman's name to me.

RUSKIN. — fosters and encourages her in her behaviour.

MR. RUSKIN. Lady Eastlake be damned.

MRS. RUSKIN. Mr. Ruskin.

MR. RUSKIN. A doctor in Hampstead! What she needs is a sound caning — the one her father never gave her, and which he, himself, deserves for sending her gadding about — and to those boarding schools, where mistresses pilfer from parents and teach daughters the most approved mode of disrespecting their husbands.

MRS. RUSKIN. Well said, indeed, Mr. Ruskin.

MR. RUSKIN. Did she ever really care for you, John? Or was it your fame — that she might make a figure of herself in society? Would a wife who truly cared for her husband seek to discomfit him before his friends, or unman him in the presence of his parents? *(There is a knock at the door.)* Yes. *(Crawley enters.)*

CRAWLEY. Mr. and Mrs. Percival Glasco are here, sir.

MR. RUSKIN. Show them into the morning room, Crawley.

RUSKIN. Crawley —

MRS. RUSKIN. John, come to the recital with us. You were always a particular favorite of the Glascos'.

RUSKIN. I'll be down in a moment, Mother. Crawley, please tell young Mrs. Ruskin I wish to see her.

CRAWLEY. Yes, sir. *(Crawley leaves.)*

MR. RUSKIN. You must be very firm, John.

MRS. RUSKIN. Remember, dear, the righteous wrath of Moses, and how he was able to set the Israelites back on the path to virtue. *(Ruskin's parents leave. He picks up Effie's sketch pad and begins to look through it. A moment later Effie enters.)*

EFFIE. Crawley said you wished to see me.

RUSKIN. I sent for you, yes. *(They stare at each other a moment.)* Why do you dishonor me before my parents, Effie?

EFFIE. John, it's they dishonor you. Dishonor us both. *(Pause.)* John, I am your wife.

RUSKIN. How is it you've come by these sketches of Millais'?

EFFIE. You know very well he gave them me in Scotland.

RUSKIN. I want you to send them back to him.

EFFIE. That is quite impossible, as I do not communicate with him in any way.

RUSKIN. I'm to believe you have not seen or written him since we left Scotland?

EFFIE. *(Plaintively.)* You know it's true.

RUSKIN. *(Moved.)* Is it, Effie? *(Effie looks thoughtfully at her husband a moment, then speaks.)*

EFFIE. John. *(Pause.)* Let's get away. The continent. We needn't wait 'til spring.

RUSKIN. Get away?

EFFIE. From this house. *(Ruskin stares at his wife sympathetically and nods.)*

RUSKIN. I suppose we might spend some time in Switzerland, before going on to Italy.

EFFIE. You could do your research in Geneva.

RUSKIN. We could stay at the hotel there — the one with the landlady who liked you so much. Austrian. What was her name?

EFFIE. Frau Flatscher.

RUSKIN. Oh, yes. The valley will be lovely this time of year.

EFFIE. Yes. *(Pause.)* Let me tell Crawley.

RUSKIN. Mother and Father first. *(Effie looks deeply apprehensive.)* What is it?

EFFIE. They will try to prevent it, John.

RUSKIN. You don't know that.

EFFIE. I think we both do.

RUSKIN. Do we? *(Pause.)* Is it Millais? This mad dash from London?

EFFIE. Why must you do this?

RUSKIN. Why must you despise them?

EFFIE. I don't despise them. I pity them.

RUSKIN. That will amuse them.

EFFIE. Will it?

RUSKIN. Father, especially.

EFFIE. As you like.

RUSKIN. As I like. Well, as I like, Mrs. Ruskin, you will return these sketches — yourself — to Millais — tomorrow.

EFFIE. No. *(Effie turns to leave.)*

RUSKIN. Mrs. Ruskin. *(Effie turns back.)* You've forgotten your sketchbook. *(Ruskin throws Effie's sketch pad into the air and it falls to the floor, pages scattering. Ruskin walks out of the room. Effie begins to pick up her sketching. Crawley very quietly enters the room and begins to help her.)*

EFFIE. I'm sorry, Crawley.

CRAWLEY. Yes, ma'am. *(Blackout.)*

Scene 3

Lights up. Early January 1854. The drawing room at Denmark Hill. Lady Eastlake is examining a painting in the room. Crawley enters.

CRAWLEY. Lady Eastlake, young Mrs. Ruskin will be with you in a moment.

LADY EASTLAKE. Thank you, Crawley. *(Crawley leaves, and Lady Eastlake returns to looking at the painting. Murmuring:)* What can he have been thinking? *(Effie enters.)*

EFFIE. Elizabeth, it is so good to see you. You look well.

LADY EASTLAKE. And you, Effie. How I've missed you, dear. *(They embrace.)* So, let me see. Well, decidedly, you have not grown fat and healthy from your time in the country. How discouraging. Why, Effie, you look as pale as Marley's ghost.

EFFIE. Elizabeth.

LADY EASTLAKE. And as miserable.

EFFIE. Shall I rattle my chains for you?

LADY EASTLAKE. I would say yes, but I fear what I might hear.

EFFIE. Come now, Elizabeth, I'm perfectly all right. What do you think of John's latest acquisition?

LADY EASTLAKE. Frankly, I think it quite mediocre.

EFFIE. Oh, but the coloring is quite pleasant and —

LADY EASTLAKE. Effie, my dress is quite pleasant, but I don't propose tacking it on your wall. Though I have no doubt if John got such a notion into his head, even my old pantalets would be hanging now in some of London's finest drawing rooms. *(Pause.)* Effie, are you sure you're all right?

EFFIE. Elizabeth, you begin to sound like Mother Ruskin, who would clap one into bed a week for blushing.

LADY EASTLAKE. That I might sound like that woman. Come now, tell me all about your trip to Scotland.

EFFIE. The Highlands were lovely — as usual — but it is good to be back among friends and the civilised comforts of London. Elizabeth, I've not yet read your essay in *The Quarterly*, though I have been told it is —

LADY EASTLAKE. The Highlands were lovely? Four months away and that is all — the Highlands were lovely?

EFFIE. Well, the weather was, as you can imagine, appalling. It nearly drove ... Sometimes I think I must be of a brooding, somber turn of mind to delight in such an atmosphere. John was ... *(Effie shrugs.)*

LADY EASTLAKE. Yes?

EFFIE. John was John.

LADY EASTLAKE. Was he? And Millais?

EFFIE. He was agreeable.

LADY EASTLAKE. Agreeable. I see. What happened in Scotland, dear? *(Effie is silent.)* Effie, I was at the Academy two days ago with

Sir Charles. You'll never guess who we saw there. Everett Millais.

EFFIE. Did you?

LADY EASTLAKE. Yes. So changed from when last I saw him.

EFFIE. Was he?

LADY EASTLAKE. Very much so. *(Pause.)* We spoke at length — the weather, art, but not a word about Scotland, he hardly mentioned John, and never you. Not once. Then I noticed how unhappy he looked, and all I could think was I wonder if Effie knows Everett Millais is in love with her.

EFFIE. *(Begins to cry.)* Please, Elizabeth.

LADY EASTLAKE. Forgive me.

EFFIE. Scotland was a nightmare.

LADY EASTLAKE. What happened?

EFFIE. I swore to John I would not come back with him.

LADY EASTLAKE. Oh, Effie.

EFFIE. How I have required all the trials I have had. *(Pause.)* In Edinburgh, there was such a clamor for him. He was priest, holy man, and god. And night after night, when they met me. The same. His wife! You are so beautiful. Of course you are. You would have to be. You would have to be. *(Pause.)* If ever one's punishment were fitted them.

LADY EASTLAKE. Why do you reproach yourself in this way?

EFFIE. How I used to exult in John's worship. His adoration.

(Mr. Ruskin enters.)

MR. RUSKIN. Good afternoon, Lady Eastlake. Pardon my interruption. Euphemia, you promised you would play at the pianoforte for John and his guest, Mr. Eliott.

EFFIE. At two o'clock, it is not yet half-past one.

MR. RUSKIN. But they are ready now.

EFFIE. But, sir, I am engaged at the moment with Lady Eastlake.

LADY EASTLAKE. You play so beautifully, Effie, I can hardly blame anyone for being overeager to hear you. Go. I will wait for you.

EFFIE. Are you sure, Elizabeth?

LADY EASTLAKE. I'm sure. Go, dear. *(Effie leaves.)*

MR. RUSKIN. I see she's been weeping. Another one of her fits?

LADY EASTLAKE. Fits?

MR. RUSKIN. Surely, Lady Eastlake, you must know that Effie is a neurasthenic, subject to sudden changes in mood and fits of inexplicable anger and depression.

LADY EASTLAKE. I assure you, sir, I know no such thing.

MR. RUSKIN. She must keep things from you then.

LADY EASTLAKE. I again assure you, you are quite mistaken. *(Mrs. Ruskin enters.)*

MRS. RUSKIN. Oh, Lady Eastlake — you're here — what a happy surprise. *(Pause.)* I had been hoping to have a word with you. *(Pause.)* I think I may presume to speak for you — so happily married yourself these past years to Sir Charles — when I say a wife should obey her husband in everything but what is against God's commandments.

LADY EASTLAKE. May I respectfully ask, madam, that you never again presume to speak for me? *(Pause.)* Especially in that curious way of yours, which seems forever to combine equal parts religion with female servitude.

MRS. RUSKIN. Lady Eastlake, your frankness of speech little becomes you, despite what your smart London friends may have led you to believe.

LADY EASTLAKE. Indeed?

MRS. RUSKIN. Indeed. Further, Lady Eastlake, I might remind you that you are a guest in my house, and —

LADY EASTLAKE. Madam, I am here at the invitation of your daughter-in-law. As her guest, and friend, I —

MR. RUSKIN. If you are indeed her friend, Lady Eastlake, you would do well to counsel her in a more sober fashion.

LADY EASTLAKE. Sober fashion?

MR. RUSKIN. It cannot have escaped your notice that Effie is deeply troubled.

LADY EASTLAKE. Unhappy, perhaps.

MR. RUSKIN. Troubled. And that if she does not exert herself now in the vigor of youth, she could well drift into dementia and insanity.

LADY EASTLAKE. Sir, I cannot believe you to be in earnest.

MR. RUSKIN. No? She is young and beautiful, but she will not always be so. Come, Lady Eastlake. We both know women in

London society — youth gone, beauty vanished — as addicted to the rouge pot as they are the spirit bottle and worse.

LADY EASTLAKE. But these are not women who have had the advantage of all the love and respect your daughter-in-law has had. But the poor miserable creatures of cold, insensitive husbands and narrow-minded intrusive families, who respect and love them only insofar as they are docile, malleable, and decorative.

MRS. RUSKIN. Lady Eastlake, having absolutely no children of your own, you can hardly guess at the effect of your fantastical notions of wifely duties upon youthful high spirits and oversensitive natures. Further, you apparently —

LADY EASTLAKE. Please! *(Pause.)* Obviously, you have both felt the need today to enlighten me. If that was your intent, please consider your duty most happily discharged, as you have given me much to reflect upon.

MR. RUSKIN. That we might enlighten anyone, Lady Eastlake, greatly humbles us. That we might enlighten you, absolutely amazes us. Mrs. Ruskin. *(Mrs. Ruskin joins her husband at the door.)* And, Lady Eastlake, while you're waiting and since you profess to have such a keen interest in art, you might want to take note of the latest addition to John's collection on the wall there. There is much talk of it now in London.

LADY EASTLAKE. I have already had a brief glance at it.

MR. RUSKIN. The work can only be properly appreciated after close inspection and much contemplation.

LADY EASTLAKE. I fear, sir, I have drained it of every possible pleasure it might have for me.

MR. RUSKIN. Good day, Lady Eastlake.

LADY EASTLAKE. Good day. *(Blackout.)*

Scene 4

Lights up. April 13, 1854. The drawing room at Denmark Hill. Everett Millais waits nervously. There is a canvas wrapped in brown paper and twine near him. Effie Ruskin enters the room and is amazed to find him there.

MILLAIS. Good afternoon ... Mrs. Ruskin. *(Effie nods.)* I'm sorry. I did not expect to see you. I wished merely to leave your husband's portrait. *(Effie nods again.)* Is he about?

EFFIE. No. He's in the City, at the Library.

MILLAIS. Oh.

EFFIE. Crawley did not tell you?

MILLAIS. No. He must have forgotten.

EFFIE. Forgotten?

MILLAIS. Absentminded as ever, I suppose.

EFFIE. I have never found him so.

MILLAIS. No? Well, there you are then.

EFFIE. I beg your pardon?

MILLAIS. Oh, good Lord, [Countess] ... Mrs. Ruskin ... you never would let me get away with anything.

EFFIE. No.

MILLAIS. Crawley told me your husband was out. I chose to wait — that I might say goodbye.

EFFIE. Goodbye?

MILLAIS. I leave for Cairo Wednesday next.

EFFIE. Cairo?

MILLAIS. To paint in the Holy Lands for four years.

EFFIE. Such a long time — so very far away.

MILLAIS. London is — I don't know. I thought something — perhaps — rather different. *(Effie nods, and there is an awkward silence.)* Well. Goodbye, then. *(Millais turns to leave; Effie speaks suddenly.)*

EFFIE. I hope you find what you're looking for in Egypt, Mr. Millais.

MILLAIS. *(With some bitterness.)* Yes, of course.

EFFIE. I'm sorry.

MILLAIS. No. I'm sorry, Countess. Forgive me. *(Millais turns to leave; Effie calls to him.)*

EFFIE. Mr. Millais. *(Millais turns back.)* God protect and watch over you always. *(Millais nods, then turns again to leave.)* Everett. *(Millais looks back, surprised.)* At night — I will whisper your name.

MILLAIS. My name?

EFFIE. You will hear me? *(Millais walks quietly over to Effie.)*

MILLAIS. Yes, Effie. *(They stand awkwardly a moment. Millais slowly leans down and kisses Effie. He takes her in his arms and they kiss passionately. Suddenly Effie pushes him away.)*

EFFIE. No. You might —

MILLAIS. What? *(Effie is silent.)* What is it? *(Ruskin can be heard outside speaking to Crawley.)*

RUSKIN. Crawley, when they arrive, please show them into the drawing room. *(Ruskin enters. He looks at Effie and Millais for a moment before speaking.)* I interrupt? *(Effie is silent. Millais looks at Ruskin, then to Effie. He studies her closely.)* A moment of surpassing cordiality? *(Effie walks out of the room.)* Come now, Everett. This infatuation of yours is the stuff of schoolboys. *(Ruskin sees the wrapped canvas by the fireplace.)* The portrait! You finished it! *(Ruskin begins to unwrap the painting.)* My God! *(Ruskin looks from the portrait to Millais, who stares at him silently.)* Truth and Nature in the very oil and pigment of it.

MILLAIS. John, you may from this moment consider any further intimacy between us as at an end.

RUSKIN. I see. *(Pause.)* Can it be, Everett, you have allowed yourself to be so completely blinded and deluded?

MILLAIS. Yes. I fear so. *(Millais walks out. Blackout.)*

Scene 5

April 14, 1854. The drawing room at Denmark Hill. The day after Everett Millais' visit. Ruskin is sitting in a chair reading. Effie enters in evening dress. She is surprised to find her husband not dressed to dine out.

EFFIE. John, tonight we dine with Sir Walter and Lady James.

RUSKIN. No, tonight *you* dine with Sir Walter and Lady James. I stopped in at Whitehall Place yesterday and told Lady James I would not be able to attend as I must dine with Mother and Father, who are having the Pritchards.

EFFIE. You never told me.

RUSKIN. There was no need. I told Lady James you would dine there tonight, by yourself, with pleasure.

EFFIE. You told her what?

RUSKIN. I believe I have made myself clear.

EFFIE. I ought, at the very least, to have been consulted.

RUSKIN. I never intend as long as my parents live to consult you on any subject of importance to them. They wish me to dine with them and the Pritchards. So I shall. You, likewise, will follow my commands implicitly and —

EFFIE. No. I will not. I will not go. I will send word to Lady James and explain to her that I cannot dine out at any large party by myself.

RUSKIN. I forbid it.

EFFIE. Nevertheless. I will no longer play the part of your neglected young wife, an object of scorn, liable to be cast by society gossips in a thousand baseless intrigues.

RUSKIN. Yesterday, as I recall, you had little difficulty playing the part. *(There is a knock at the door.)* Yes. *(Crawley enters.)* Yes, Crawley.

CRAWLEY. Lady Eastlake is here, ma'am.

EFFIE. *(Looking surprised.)* Thank you, Crawley. Please show her in. *(Crawley leaves.)*

RUSKIN. I told you I did not want that woman in this house. If you do not go tonight, write your friend Mrs. Bishop in Germany, and tell her you will not be allowed to join her next month as you had planned.

EFFIE. Very well. I will write her directly.

RUSKIN. The only thing for you is a good beating with a common stick. *(Lady Eastlake enters.)* Lady Eastlake. *(Ruskin walks out of the room.)*

LADY EASTLAKE. How that man loathes me.

EFFIE. Elizabeth, he —

LADY EASTLAKE. It's of no consequence.

EFFIE. Forgive me, Elizabeth, I'm rather distracted at the moment. The trip to Germany, and —

LADY EASTLAKE. Yes, when do you leave?

EFFIE. Actually — soon. *(Lady Eastlake nods.)*

LADY EASTLAKE. Everyone, it seems, is off somewhere. Millais stopped in last evening. Apparently bound for Cairo.

EFFIE. Oh?

LADY EASTLAKE. Yes. *(Effie is silent.)* I told Sir Charles I simply must get away as well. Italy perhaps. *(Effie nods.)* What an entire Vesuvius, Millais! He can hardly have drawn a placid breath all his life.

EFFIE. I saw him yesterday. Did he tell you?

LADY EASTLAKE. Yes.

EFFIE. I can't imagine what he made of my odd behaviour.

LADY EASTLAKE. He is concerned.

EFFIE. You may assure him I am quite well.

LADY EASTLAKE. Effie, Everett Millais asked that I speak with you. He is quite convinced you —

EFFIE. Elizabeth, Everett Millais is in — has lost his head — you must make sure, for his sake, that he —

LADY EASTLAKE. Effie, is it true John keeps a journal in which he records —

EFFIE. One of his eccentricities. Nothing.

LADY EASTLAKE. Nothing?

EFFIE. Elizabeth, I know you can not possibly mean to pry.

LADY EASTLAKE. No, Effie. But, I must know what it is goes on here.

EFFIE. I see. You would pry then. You will forgive me, Elizabeth, if, under the circumstances, I tell you I must bid you good day.

LADY EASTLAKE. What is it, Effie?

EFFIE. I assure you I —

LADY EASTLAKE. No, Effie. Not with me.

EFFIE. Good day. *(Effie turns to leave.)*

LADY EASTLAKE. It's John, isn't it? *(Pause.)* With his spying and his writing down every little —

EFFIE. No, Elizabeth. Not John. Me. *(Pause.)* Why do you think he despises me so?

LADY EASTLAKE. Why should John despise you? *(Effie is silent.)* Why, Effie?

EFFIE. He — he believes I deceived him.

LADY EASTLAKE. Did you, Effie? *(Effie is silent.)* In Scotland?

EFFIE. No. Years ago.

LADY EASTLAKE. Years ago? When you first married? *(Effie looks away.)* Something you did not tell John?

EFFIE. It was John told me.

LADY EASTLAKE. He told you? *(Effie is silent.)* You were ignorant of something plainly apparent to John?

EFFIE. Elizabeth, I didn't know.

LADY EASTLAKE. How is that possible? *(Effie is silent.)* Effie?

EFFIE. I didn't, Elizabeth, I —

LADY EASTLAKE. Forgive me, Effie, but —

EFFIE. I didn't know. What young girl on her wedding night —

LADY EASTLAKE. Your wedding night? *(Pause.)* What did John tell you?

EFFIE. No, Elizabeth.

LADY EASTLAKE. What, Effie?

EFFIE. I can't.

LADY EASTLAKE. You must tell me, Effie.

EFFIE. He saw — I have a disease.

LADY EASTLAKE. A disease? *(Pause.)* What sort of disease? *(Effie still does not respond. Taking Effie by the arm with great*

59

urgency:) Effie, I am a doctor's daughter, I have not been raised in ignorance, nor have I been taught to call ignorance delicacy, what sort of disease is this?

EFFIE. I'm not sure. A kind of women's disease.

LADY EASTLAKE. A women's disease. I see. Very well. I will be blunt with you, Effie, and I want you to be equally blunt with me. Do you have pain? Sores? *(Effie is silent.)* Is there any cramping? Burning?

EFFIE. Elizabeth. Please!

LADY EASTLAKE. Effie, you may go to a physician, he will only ask the same, and I think you would rather speak to me of these things than to a doctor. Now, I'm sorry to have to ask you this, but I must. Is this disease aggravated when you have relations with John?

EFFIE. ... relations with John.

LADY EASTLAKE. I'm sorry, I know how trying this must be for you, Effie, so intimate is the union between husband and wife —

EFFIE. Stop, Elizabeth! You must stop!

LADY EASTLAKE. Effie. *(Slowly the expression on Lady Eastlake's face changes.)* Oh, Effie. You have never had relations.

EFFIE. Our wedding night, he drew off my nightdress — turned — that horrible look — because — he said — he saw my body was diseased — foul —

LADY EASTLAKE. Foul!

EFFIE. — that I might bathe — never enough —

LADY EASTLAKE. Effie, this is madness.

EFFIE. — and so formed as would disgust any man.

LADY EASTLAKE. *(Moving towards Effie to comfort her.)* No, dear. No.

EFFIE. *(Cowering from Lady Eastlake.)* No, Elizabeth! Don't come near me. You will see it is all in fact true. I could not stand it if you too should turn from me.

LADY EASTLAKE. Oh, Effie.

EFFIE. No! Elizabeth, please, I'm begging you — please don't — please — please — *(Lady Eastlake moves quickly to embrace Effie, by now completely overwrought and offering no further resistance.)*

LADY EASTLAKE. There now, dear. There's nothing wrong with you. *(Blackout.)*

Scene 6

Lights up. April 25, 1854. The drawing room at Denmark Hill. Effie Ruskin moves about the room nervously. In the center of the room are a satchel and a black leather bag. There is a knock at the door.

EFFIE. Yes. *(Crawley enters.)* Yes, Crawley?
CRAWLEY. Ma'am, your parents will be waiting for you at Hitchen, the first stop after the train leaves King's Cross. Your mother will get on with you there for Perth and your father will take the next train up to London.
EFFIE. Yes, Crawley, anything else?
CRAWLEY. Yes, *(Taking a letter from his jacket.)* Ma'am. A letter from your mother.
EFFIE. Crawley, thank you. If they should ever find out — if you should ever suffer because of this — or if you are ever in need of any kind, you will contact me.
CRAWLEY. Yes, ma'am.
EFFIE. Promise me.
CRAWLEY. Yes, ma'am.
EFFIE. I will always be in your debt, Crawley. Always.
CRAWLEY. I would do anything for you, ma'am. *(Crawley leaves. Effie begins to read the letter from her mother. Ruskin enters. Effie quickly hides the letter.)*
RUSKIN. Frank will be some time getting the carriage, so you might as well sit and wait. *(Effie paces nervously.)* Take your ease, Mrs. Ruskin, you will be free of me soon enough. *(Effie sits down. Ruskin notices Effie's luggage.)* Two little bags. How like you, Effie. Do you think I don't know about the trunks you've sent to Bow-

erswell. Trunks for a three-month stay. *(Effie stiffens slightly.)* Is there someone in Scotland for you to captivate — Millais perhaps — is that why you're so keen to be off, or is it you plan to give your sisters a fashion show with their lesson? *(Ruskin, noticing Effie is nervously preoccupied, pauses a moment.)* Effie, when you return in August from Bowerswell you had better regained what little self-composure you had. *(Pause.)* These fits of fretfulness. Your irritability and sullenness these past few days have been intolerable. You will change, Mrs. Ruskin, and return, if not the affectionate, tractable wife I'd once hoped, then at least a calmer, less distracting one. *(Effie turns and stares at her husband with a look of absolute hatred.)* Do you think I care you despise me? Do you? Answer me. *(Effie walks over by the window and stands with her back to her husband.)*

EFFIE. *(Murmuring.)* God, be with me.

RUSKIN. What was that you said? What? *(Effie does not respond.)* Answer me! Answer me! *(Effie does not respond.)* Nothing at all. Mad. My wife is mad. *(Pause.)* Wife? She is not a wife. A wife gives comfort to her husband. Not a creator of discord between her husband and his parents. Wife? Did she tend to her husband's needs? Help him in his work? Did she once suffer to keep her opinions to herself? Wife? Did she ever seek to soothe rather than irritate, pacify rather than engage, or to be unassuming and modest instead of proud.

EFFIE. You dare ask what kind of wife I've been? You, who have sought to degrade and compromise me in any and every way you could. Who have tried to rob me of my dignity — my very reason.

RUSKIN. It isn't so.

EFFIE. I'm trying not to hate you, John.

RUSKIN. Hate me?

EFFIE. I pray God keep me from hating you.

RUSKIN. You hardly know what you say. Your mind grows weaker and more disorganised daily. Yes. As your body sickens and corrupts. *(Effie rises quickly.)*

EFFIE. Crawley! *(Ruskin flies at his wife, taking her by the arm.)*

RUSKIN. I will break you, Effie. *(Effie looks deeply into her hus-*

band's eyes a moment, then quietly takes his hand from her arm. *Crawley enters.)*

EFFIE. Crawley. Please take my bags. I am ready to go. *(Crawley takes Effie's bags. Effie turns and looks at her husband one last time, then walks out of the room followed by Crawley. Blackout.)*

Scene 7

Lights up. April 25, 1854. The drawing room at Denmark Hill, quarter-to-six on the evening of Effie Ruskin's departure.

MR. RUSKIN. Strange, but Frank swears he saw the Grays yesterday in Bury, Saint James, talking to Lady Eastlake of all people.

MRS. RUSKIN. Effie's parents? But, they don't know Lady Eastlake.

MR. RUSKIN. I know. It couldn't have been them. But, then, you know Frank. *(Mr. Ruskin motions as if drinking from a bottle. Mrs. Ruskin nods knowingly.)* Unless of course they thought since their daughter was leaving London for Perth, there could be no better reason, than that they should leave Perth for London.

MRS. RUSKIN. Imagine it, Mr. Ruskin. The Grays in fearful flight from their mad daughter, arriving in London, only to be cornered in Bury Street by that tigress in petticoats.

MR. RUSKIN. The twice-blessed George and Sophia Gray.

MRS. RUSKIN. What luck, her sisters' governess eloping, and her mother having to call Effie home.

MR. RUSKIN. Eloped! She probably ran shrieking from that madhouse, where all the children are impolite, and the young girls are as liable as the young boys to be pitching stones and hanging out of trees.

MRS. RUSKIN. Like little monkeys, I daresay.

MR. RUSKIN. Mother, you are wicked.

63

MRS. RUSKIN. Where is John?

MR. RUSKIN. There was someone at the door for him. A newspaperman, I believe.

MRS. RUSKIN. Another one? Oh, but, Mr. Ruskin, he does not like fame. He said to me today: Mother, they want to know everything about me. They ask what it is I have for dinner, and when I tell them chops, they say — Mr. Ruskin, what is it you do with the bones? *(The Ruskins laugh. Ruskin enters the room. He is carrying a citation and a packet in his hand, and looks stricken. His father does not, at first, notice.)*

MR. RUSKIN. And what did they want to know now, John, of the "Edinburgh Sensation"? Your favorite brand of tooth powder?

MRS. RUSKIN. John, what is it?

RUSKIN. Effie has served me with a citation to court.

MR. RUSKIN. *(Grabbing the citation from his son's hand.)* What! Let me see that. *(He begins to read the citation.)*

MRS. RUSKIN. A citation to court? Whatever for?

RUSKIN. To — to nullify our marriage.

MRS. RUSKIN. A divorce? No, John. You must not blame yourself for this. Effie has brought this ruin down upon herself and upon her family. We all knew — always — that when opposed, she was capable of taking any step which —

RUSKIN. Not a divorce, Mother.

MRS. RUSKIN. I don't understand.

RUSKIN. *(Handing the packet to his mother.)* This, she addressed to you.

MRS. RUSKIN. To me? *(She takes the packet and opens it. She removes a set of keys and a small book. She holds them up.)* Effie's keys and her account book. *(She puts them down on a nearby table then reaches into the packet again and takes out a ring.)* Effie's wedding ring. *(She puts the wedding ring down on the table and reaches into the packet and takes out a letter addressed to herself. She looks again from her son to her husband, then opens the letter.)* My dear Mrs. Ruskin, You are aware that I was married by the Scottish form in my father's house on the tenth of April, eighteen forty-eight. From that day to this your son has never made me his wife. *(Mrs. Ruskin looks up from the letter.)* What on earth can she mean? *(Neither man responds, and she continues reading silently. Gradually, the look on her face changes as she begins to realise the accusation being made against her son. She slowly lowers the letter as she finishes it, speaking the last words in a monotone.)* I remain yours truly, Euphemia C. Gray. *(All three are silent. Mr. Ruskin finally speaks.)*

MR. RUSKIN. What can be her purpose in making so scurrilous a charge?

MRS. RUSKIN. It is evil. I would not have thought her capable of it.

MR. RUSKIN. But, to lie in such a way. Why, John? *(Ruskin is silent. Holding up the citation:)* It can't be true, John.

MRS. RUSKIN. Mr. Ruskin!

RUSKIN. She will stop at nothing. If it means destroying me, she will stop at nothing.

MRS. RUSKIN. There.

MR. RUSKIN. But, when there were no children, John, you said —

RUSKIN. Of course there were no children, Father! Effie a mother? It's laughable. We know that.

MR. RUSKIN. John, is what she is claiming true?

RUSKIN. She has only taken this course so that she will be free to marry Millais. That's all she wants. This is —

MRS. RUSKIN. All a lie.

MR. RUSKIN. *(Furiously.)* Did you, or did you not ever have relations with your wife!

RUSKIN. Father —

MRS. RUSKIN. Mr. Ruskin.

MR. RUSKIN. John!

RUSKIN. No. *(The echo of his abject "no" reverberates in the stillness of the room. Father, mother, and son all look away from one another. Finally, Ruskin speaks.)* Sometimes I fear I have no heart for anything, but paint, canvas, and stone. *(Pause.)* Shortly after we were married, I found her crying upstairs. *(Pause.)* Did I tell you? *(Ruskin's parents stare at him silently.)* No, I don't believe I did. One of my diaries. I'll find it for you. I tried to comfort her, of course, in a dutiful way — as would have pleased you both.

But for myself, I own, I felt nothing — absolutely nothing. *(Pause.)* No, Effie, I whispered softly, trying to calm her — we must live as the saints. No, Effie —

MR. RUSKIN. John.

RUSKIN. *(Seeming not to hear his father.)* — since you have professed a dislike to me in the past, it would be sinful now to enter into a fleshly connection with you.

MR. RUSKIN. John!

RUSKIN. No, Effie, you might have children, and as you are — quite insane — unfit to bring them up.

MRS. RUSKIN. Oh, Mr. Ruskin.

MR. RUSKIN. Stop it, John.

RUSKIN. No, Effie, you disgust me. No, Effie, you revolt me. No —

MRS. RUSKIN. John. No, John —

MR. RUSKIN. *(Outraged.)* We will not listen to this.

RUSKIN. — Effie, I am afraid.

MR. RUSKIN. Stop it at once!

RUSKIN. Effie, I'm frightened of your woman's body —

MR. RUSKIN. I said, that's enough!

MRS. RUSKIN. Oh, John, please don't.

RUSKIN. — I am terrified of your woman's love.

MRS. RUSKIN. *(Weeping.)* John, stop. Please stop. Please.

RUSKIN. No, Effie. No, Effie. Please, no, Effie.

MR. RUSKIN. John, you are hurting your mother.

RUSKIN. Am I? *(Mr. Ruskin goes to comfort his wife.)* I'm sorry, Mama, I don't mean to hurt you. I know you both would do anything for me. Would sacrifice your very lives for me. But, don't you see — don't you understand, I *have* sacrificed my life for you.

MR. RUSKIN. That's not true, John.

RUSKIN. But, it is, Father. It is. And in vain. All in vain. For you see I am once more — as I have always truly been — completely and utterly alone. Effie — please don't do this. Please believe that I love you.

MR. RUSKIN. Where's your dignity, man?

RUSKIN. Father, I —

MR. RUSKIN. Not another word! *(Ruskin is silent.)* We will put away the past. We must think of your future now. We will go at once and see my solicitor.

MRS. RUSKIN. Everything will be all right, John. We will, the three of us, face this together.

MR. RUSKIN. Yes. Never mind. You did nothing wrong. You found at once she had no love for you, and lived with her accordingly. That is all we will say. That is all anyone need ever know.

End of Act Two

EPILOGUE

VOICE. Lady Millais. *(No response.)* Lady Millais. *(No response.)* Effie. Yes, come. The Queen will see you now.

The End

PROPERTY LIST

Props to suggest drawing room at Denmark Hill
Props to suggest Alex Stewart's cottage
Props to suggest the Philosophical Institution at Edinburgh
Writing paper and pen or pencil
Trunks and suitcases with various things to unpack (CRAWLEY)
Notes (RUSKIN)
Clothes (EFFIE)
Small book (RUSKIN)
Sketch pad (MILLAIS)
Plaid blanket (RUSKIN)
Bouquet of foxgloves (EFFIE)
Glass container (EFFIE)
Pitcher of water (EFFIE)
Scissors (EFFIE)
Small chair (MILLAIS)
Sewing (EFFIE)
Bonnet and jacket (EFFIE)
Sketch pad (EFFIE)
Piece of cloth (EFFIE)
Book (MILLAIS)
Canvas with cover (MILLAIS)
Plaid blanket (MILLAIS)
Comb (EFFIE)
Towel (EFFIE)
Small trunk (MILLAIS)
Newspaper (EFFIE)
Clippings of hair (EFFIE)
Satchel (MILLAIS)
Tray with decanter and four glasses (CRAWLEY)
Canvas wrapped in brown paper and twine (RUSKIN)
Book (RUSKIN)
Letter (CRAWLEY)
Satchel and black leather bag (CRAWLEY)
Citation (RUSKIN)
Packet with keys, small book, wedding ring, and letter (RUSKIN)

SOUND EFFECTS

Wild applause
Rain
Crowd

Brig O'Turk, Scotland

NEW PLAYS

★ **AS BEES IN HONEY DROWN by Douglas Carter Beane.** Winner of the John Gassner Playwriting Award. A hot young novelist finds the subject of his new screenplay in a New York socialite who leads him into the world of *Auntie Mame* and *Breakfast at Tiffany's*, before she takes him for a ride. "A delicious soufflé of a satire … [an] extremely entertaining fable for an age that always chooses image over substance." *–The NY Times* "… A witty assessment of one of the most active and relentless industries in a consumer society … the creation of 'hot' young things, which the media have learned to mass produce with efficiency and zeal." *–The NY Daily News* [3M, 3W, flexible casting] ISBN: 0-8222-1651-5

★ **STUPID KIDS by John C. Russell.** In rapid, highly stylized scenes, the story follows four high-school students as they make their way from first through eighth period and beyond, struggling with the fears, frustrations, and longings peculiar to youth. "In STUPID KIDS … playwright John C. Russell gets the opera of adolescence to a T … The stylized teenspeak of STUPID KIDS … suggests that Mr. Russell may have hidden a tape recorder under a desk in study hall somewhere and then scoured the tapes for good quotations … it is the kids' insular, ceaselessly churning world, a pre-adult world of Doritos and libidos, that the playwright seeks to lay bare." *–The NY Times* "STUPID KIDS [is] a sharp-edged … whoosh of teen angst and conformity anguish. It is also very funny." *–NY Newsday* [2M, 2W] ISBN: 0-8222-1698-1

★ **COLLECTED STORIES by Donald Margulies.** From Obie Award-winner Donald Margulies comes a provocative analysis of a student-teacher relationship that turns sour when the protégé becomes a rival. "With his fine ear for detail, Margulies creates an authentic, insular world, and he gives equal weight to the opposing viewpoints of two formidable characters." *–The LA Times* "This is probably Margulies' best play to date …" *–The NY Post* "… always fluid and lively, the play is thick with ideas, like a stock-pot of good stew." *–The Village Voice* [2W] ISBN: 0-8222-1640-X

★ **FREEDOMLAND by Amy Freed.** An overdue showdown between a son and his father sets off fireworks that illuminate the neurosis, rage and anxiety of one family – and of America at the turn of the millennium. "FREEDOMLAND's more obvious links are to *Buried Child* and *Bosoms and Neglect*. Freed, like Guare, is an inspired wordsmith with a gift for surreal touches in situations grounded in familiar and real territory." *–Curtain Up* [3M, 4W] ISBN: 0-8222-1719-8

★ **STOP KISS by Diana Son.** A poignant and funny play about the ways, both sudden and slow, that lives can change irrevocably. "There's so much that is vital and exciting about STOP KISS … you want to embrace this young author and cheer her onto other works … the writing on display here is funny and credible … you also will be charmed by its heartfelt characters and up-to-the-minute humor." *–The NY Daily News* "… irresistibly exciting … a sweet, sad, and enchantingly sincere play." *–The NY Times* [3M, 3W] ISBN: 0-8222-1731-7

★ **THREE DAYS OF RAIN by Richard Greenberg.** The sins of fathers and mothers make for a bittersweet elegy in this poignant and revealing drama. "… a work so perfectly judged it heralds the arrival of a major playwright … Greenberg is extraordinary." *–The NY Daily News* "Greenberg's play is filled with graceful passages that are by turns melancholy, harrowing, and often, quite funny." *–Variety* [2M, 1W] ISBN: 0-8222-1676-0

★ **THE WEIR by Conor McPherson.** In a bar in rural Ireland, the local men swap spooky stories in an attempt to impress a young woman from Dublin who recently moved into a nearby "haunted" house. However, the tables are soon turned when she spins a yarn of her own. "You shed all sense of time at this beautiful and devious new play." *–The NY Times* "Sheer theatrical magic. I have rarely been so convinced that I have just seen a modern classic. Tremendous." *–The London Daily Telegraph* [4M, 1W] ISBN: 0-8222-1706-6

DRAMATISTS PLAY SERVICE, INC.
440 Park Avenue South, New York, NY 10016 212-683-8960 Fax 212-213-1539
postmaster@dramatists.com www.dramatists.com